How To Defend Yourself Against Your Lawyer

more importantly
How To Avoid The Problem In The First Place

by AMELIA E. POHL, ESQ.

D1570587

EAGLE PUBLISHING COMPANY OF BOCA

EAGLE PUBLISHING COMPANY OF BOCA
4199 N. Dixie Highway, #2
Boca Raton, FL   33431
e-mail info@eaglepublishing.com

Printed in the United States of America
ISBN 1-892407-57-4
Library of Congress Catalog Card Number 2004107423

Dedication

To my brother, Fred Adinolfi.
The youngest of our "sibs," yet there is much we learn from him.

HOW TO DEFEND YOURSELF AGAINST YOUR LAWYER

TABLE OF CONTENTS

About This Book

Too often people spend more for legal counsel than they should. They pay much for mediocre advice, or worse yet, a premium price for poor advice. The problem arises because the general public is not knowledgeable about the practice of law. They don't know what they are "buying." Even if they understand the nature of their legal problem, they do not know how to choose the right "seller" of legal advice.

Many people have become so disillusioned with the legal profession that they seek to do their own legal work for common transactions such as forming a corporation, getting a divorce, preparing a Will. There are any number of legal kits can be purchased to help people with these transactions. Companies have been springing up to assist people in completing legal forms.

But not all legal problems lend themselves to self-help. If the self-help enthusiast makes a mistake, it can cost him more than if he sought legal counsel in the first place.

This book was written to help the reader know when he needs an attorney and how to choose an attorney that will solve his problem for a reasonable price. The book explains what to expect from your lawyer, and what to do if that lawyer does not live up to those expectations.

GLOSSARY

This book is designed for the average reader. Legal terminology has been kept to a minimum. There is a glossary at the end of the book in the event you come across a legal term that is not familiar to you.

FICTITIOUS NAMES AND EVENTS

The examples in this book are based loosely on actual events; however, all names are fictitious and the events, as portrayed, are fictitious.

MALE GENDER USED

The author was a feminist before she even knew that there was such a thing. But she is also an author with little patience for interrupting the flow of an idea with he/she, him/her, (s)he, and other methods of indicating that the message applies equally to male and female.

She used the masculine gender wherever appropriate, with the understanding that the point applies to men and women alike. All of the hypothetical lawyers are male, but we acknowledge that a female lawyer can behave as well (or as badly) as any male.

About the Author

Before becoming an attorney in 1985, AMELIA E. POHL taught mathematics on both the high school and college level. During her tenure as Associate Professor of Mathematics at Prince George's Community College in Maryland, she wrote several books including

Probability: A Set Theory Approach
Principals of Counting
Common Stock Sense.

She received her Juris Doctorate from the Nova University School of Law and went directly into practice, concentrating in real property, estate planning and Elder Law.

Since 1999 Amelia E. Pohl has been using her background as teacher, author and attorney to provide information to the general public about the legal system in the form of two series of books that she has written. The *Guiding Those Left Behind* series explains how to settle the estate of someone who dies. Because probate laws are state specific, she wrote different books for different states. For each book, she was assisted by an experienced attorney who practiced within the given state.

Her second series of books entitled *A Will Is Not Enough* is a continuation of the Guiding series. The Guiding series explains the problems that can occur when someone dies. The Will series explains how a person can arrange his affairs so that his family will not face similar challenges.

While writing these two series, Amelia was drawn into a law suit involving property inherited from her father. She was surprised at how many times she was mislead by attorneys who were supposed to be on her side. She wondered if she, a lawyer, could be "taken," what chance does the person with no legal background have?

This book is the result of those concerns. She wrote it to expose the ills of our legal system. She also wrote the book to suggest ways to improve thatsystem. But her primary goal was to alert readers to potential problems when seeking legal representation and how to defend against those problems.

THE COVER ARTIST

The cover art on this book was done by RAY RUSSOTTO. Ray is a longtime South Florida resident who has contributed to a number of publications in his career as a cartoonist/ illustrator. Among them are the Sun-Sentinel, the Miami Herald, New Times, Mutual Funds Magazine and Jazziz. His editorial cartoons are a regular feature in the Boca Raton News.

For more samples or contact information visit his web site.
http://www.cartoonsbyray.com

SPECIAL THANKS

This book could not have been written without the encouragement and assistance of the following people who were kind enough to take the time and effort to review the book and offer constructive criticism:

ANN ADINOLFI, FRED ADINOLFI, PAUL ADINOLFI

RALPH BEHR, MARGOT BOSCHE

NANCY SIMONYI DAVIS, JOSEPH DE STASIO

AUDRA GERBEN, ROBERT HUDEN, RUTH HUDEN

ANDREW LUCAS, FRANK LUCAS, FRANK A. LUCAS

LOUISE LUCAS, STEPHANIE LUCAS

CAROL PLANTHABER, JOHN RICHARDS

JACK C. ROLLINS, EDITH SPENCER RYAN,

MARIA SIMONYI, GEORGINA STATHAKIS

and ANN WATERWORTH.

Preface

WHAT DOCTORS AND LAWYERS HAVE IN COMMON

Used to be that when a doctor told a patient what was wrong and wrote out a prescription. The patient followed the doctor's advice. He did not questioned whether he in fact suffered from whatever disease the doctor said he had. He never thought to ask whether he really needed the medicine prescribed or whether it was the best medicine for him. If the medicine didn't make him feel better he would either go back and get a different prescription, or go see another doctor.

Enter the information age. Now we have television programs, both documentary and fictional, telling all about different diseases and the best way to treat the disease. Newspapers have weekly medical columns written by a doctor to answer questions sent in by readers. Newscasts give the latest break-through in medicine. We are inundated with television commercials that tell what drugs are available for common ills. They also caution against side effects — some of which are so unpleasant you wonder whether it wouldn't be better to just suffer the disease.

Today you can go to the Internet, type in your symptoms and get a wealth of information about what might be ailing you and what treatments are out there.

Law is not far behind medicine. Television has fictional and documentary programs that explain your legal rights. Many states broadcast meetings of their state legislature. Each state has a web site that explains certain areas of the law. Most state web sites offer information about state taxes, unclaimed property, crime victim compensation, vital records, motor vehicle registration and the state medical assistance program.

FATHER DOESN'T KNOW BEST

As any older physician will tell you, today's middle aged patient is different than his parent. The patient's parent had great faith in his doctor. Today's patient is not so trusting. He has lots of information available to him. With a relatively small amount of effort he can learn all he wants to know about whatever ails him. Not only is today's patient different, so too is today's doctor. The "father knows best" attitude is giving way to shared decisions. If different treatments are available, today's doctor is more likely to explain to the patient what is involved in the treatment, the probability of its success, and then let the patient decide which path he wants to follow.

This is not the usual case with lawyers. The paternalistic approach remains the rule. If there is more than one legal path the client can follow, too often the lawyer explains only the path he thinks best, leading the client to believe that he has no other choice.

People hesitate to question the lawyer's judgment because they are not familiar with state law. While medicine is universal, law is state specific. We all have human bodies. We can look up mankind's ills on the Internet. If the doctor says your pressure is high, you can find an explanation of high blood pressure and suggested treatments on the Web. The information you find on the subject is the same no matter where you live. This is not the case with the law. Each state has its own set of statutes. Even federal laws such as bankruptcy and Medicaid law are applied differently state to state because federal law gives the states a certain amount of leeway in the administration of the law.

Because of the complexity of the law, many thinking folk still trust their attorney to decide the best way to go. But, as many have found from unhappy experience, that trust can be misplaced. Father still doesn't know best. You need to know what is best for you. The proper role of the attorney needs to evolve to that of the doctor; namely the primary job of the attorney should be to explain your options and then let you decide what you wish to do.

The purpose of this book is to encourage the reader to become proactive in his legal representation. We will suggest questions to ask your attorney. We will explain how to evaluate the answers he gives and how to find information that will help you decide what is right for you.

MR. PERFECT LAWYER   1

The best way to defend yourself against a lawyer is not to employ a bad attorney in the first place. In this chapter we discuss the qualities of Mr. Perfect Lawyer so you know what to look for when you need a lawyer. Once you know the ideal, you can compare your lawyer to Mr. Perfect, and decide whether he is performing up to a reasonably normal standard.

What's Normal?

Those of us who suffered through a statistics course learned about the Normal Curve.

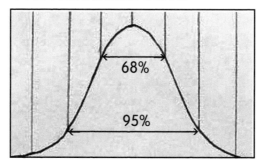

We learned that in a normal population most of the population lies in the middle, with approximately 2.5% of the population at the extreme high end and 2.5% percent at the low end. What is so interesting about the Normal Curve is that it can be applied to just about any large population.

For example, if you take the height of 100 women picked at random, you will find that most are similar in height. You can expect two or three to be much shorter than the rest and two or three to be much taller.

This same Normal Curve applies to lawyers. If you take 100 lawyers and rate them for knowledge, honesty, conscientiousness and loyalty to clients, you will find that most of them fall in the middle. You will probably find a couple that are really bad. You wonder how they passed the Bar, and as for honesty, it's just a matter of time before the state catches up to them and takes their license away.

Expect two of the hundred lawyers to be great. Smart, skilled at the area of law they practice, absolutely honest and loyal to their clients. In other words, MR. PERFECT LAWYER. All the rest aren't all that bad (with the exception of the two at the other end) but they are no Mr. Perfect either.

The question is how do you know if you're employing a gem, or a piece of glass?

Lawyers, like everyone else, give clues as to their true nature. You just need to know where and how to look. First impressions are important. When meeting an attorney for the first time make note of his looks and vocabulary.

LOOKS

A woman had two daughters, both with the same father, but very different in looks and personality. The eldest was an outstanding beauty. The younger daughter, Jan, was good-looking, but paled next to her radiant sibling. When Jan reached puberty she felt like her sister had been given all of the good genes and she got whatever was left over. Her gangly arms and legs seemed too long for her body. When she came down with a stubborn case of acne, it seemed like more than she could bear.

Jan's mother tried to comfort her. "Your sister may be good-looking, but beauty has its price. People don't want to know her for who she is. They are attracted to her for how she looks. She doesn't need to develop her personality. People will always be drawn to her just as they are to a beautiful actress on a movie screen. But looks won't make her good, kind, or interesting. These are important qualities which she may never be motivated to develop. She may grow up to be just as flat as that image on a screen."

Jan thought for moment and said "No, I'd rather be beautiful."

And that's the way it is. We all want to be beautiful. We all are attracted to handsome people. But is an attorney who is outstandingly handsome going to be your Mr. Perfect Lawyer? Probably not. It is just as the mother said, people who are extremely good-looking get ahead because of their looks.

If you are seeking to employ someone from a large law firm and the attorney is a beauty, chances are the firm employed that lawyer over another with higher grades or greater experience. The same applies to an attorney with overt sex appeal. You will want to avoid a female attorney dressed in high heels, short skirt and provocative blouse. Such an attorney has her mind elsewhere. You are paying your lawyer to solve your legal problem. You need someone with a businesslike attitude and demeanor.

When rating your attorney do not give him a "plus" for great looks or sex appeal, but rather a "minus" until he proves that he is more than a pretty face. Use similar reasoning for the opposite end of the normal curve. Don't discount an attorney because he is not a looker. One of the finest lawyers I ever met fell into that category. His father started their law practice. The father was a tall, good-looking man with a full head of wavy, white hair. When he retired his son took over. Those who had employed the father were referred to the son. The initial meeting gave most people a start. Sonny looked nothing like his father. He was short, stocky, bald and spoke with a slight lisp. Those who got past his looks were in for a pleasant surprise. Sonny was knowledgeable, honest, conscientious, and unpretentious. All in all an excellent attorney.

Give an attorney a "plus" for poor looks and no sex appeal. He used his brains and talent to get him where he is.

VOCABULARY

One way a "Professional" distinguishes himself from a "Non-professional" is to develop a complex vocabulary. The more technical the terminology, the more impressed the Non-professional is that the Professional is truly learned and worthy of great compensation. Computer techno-gobbledegook is the latest entry into the field of Professional language. We are now encountering Computer Professionals, whose fees are commensurate with such complex verbal skills.

Physicians have long understood the language advantage and adopted the long-dead Latin language as the basis of their Professional language. It remains today. Attorneys also use the no-longer-spoken Latin liberally. For example, they use the Latin term "fiduciary" to describe their relationship with their client. It could just as easily be described as a relationship of trust.

If any lawyer is reading this book, no doubt he will protest. "You know fiduciary means a lot more than having a relationship of trust. The fiduciary relationship between a lawyer and his client is a confidential relationship. Anything the client tells the lawyer is to be kept private. It is a relationship in which the lawyer is required to put the client's best interest ahead of his own best interest. Now that's what fiduciary means!"

We agree that many technical terms are short-hand for fairly complicated thoughts. There are valid, non-monetary reasons to use technical terms, such as communication with other people in the field. It is better to use a technical word or phrase to represent a complex thought when giving a lecture to other professionals or when writing a learned article. But legalese should not be used just to impress a client with the lawyer's superior knowledge, or worse yet when drafting a document that the client must sign on faith because he hasn't a clue as to what it means.

There is no reason for an attorney to use technical terms about during your initial consultation. This is the time for him to speak in plain English to let you know what he can do to help you solve your legal problem. If he is using legal terms to impress you, it may mean he is insecure about his legal knowledge or skills. If he doesn't have faith in his legal ability, why should you have faith in him?

A lawyer might be talking legalese to you because he is too learned to "come down to your level." He is so used to thinking in legal terms that it may not occur to him that you don't know what he's talking about. He is not the guy to employ to draft legal documents for you to sign. Expect his drafts to be even more confusing than his speech. It is doubtful that he will have the time, patience, or inclination to explain the meaning and legal consequences of each paragraph of the document.

Give your lawyer a "minus" for every time he uses an unfamiliar term during your initial consultation.

Once you have made a mental check of his looks and vocabulary the next thing to check out is his knowledge and experience.

KNOWLEDGE

You may wonder why it is necessary to check out your lawyer's knowledge. After all, he had to go to law school and pass a test in order to be licensed to practice law. He must be very smart. Right? Wrong! Some law schools need to fill seats, so they settle for students at the lower end of the LSAT (Law School Admission Test). And a law degree is not in the same league as one in math or science. Those who studied high school algebra, geometry or chemistry should be able to recall the mental gymnastics they had to perform just to understand basic principals. Imagine pursuing an advanced degree in math or science. Now that is reaching for concepts!

The study of law is not anything like that. All a law student needs are good verbal skills. He needs to be able to read quickly and extract the "meat" of the material, i.e., understand what he is reading. His writing needs to be well organized and his thoughts clearly expressed. He needs to be able to "think on his feet" meaning that he can develop and express his ideas so that others understand what he is trying to get across.

In other words, all he needs is the verbal skills of a high school senior with a "B" average in English.

No doubt the skeptics will protest "Oh come now. The LSAT is really hard. And so are the tests one must pass in order to be licensed to practice law."

That's true; but it doesn't take a mental giant to pass them. All that is required is time and money. The student must be willing to put in long hours studying for the test. Work books that give questions and answers to past LSAT tests are available at any book store. The student must be willing to spend the time pouring over past tests to learn the "right answers."

Once he finishes law school, he may need to pay for special classes to prepare him for the state licensing examination. These preparation classes make the student "test wise." They teach the student how to budget his time so that he gets the most points in the shortest period of time. They explain how to decide on the best choice when given two equally enticing multiple choice selections.

If the student doesn't pass the first time, he can try, try again.

The attorney you are interviewing may have graduated at the bottom of one of those "let's just fill seats" schools of law. It may have taken him two or three attempts at the licensing exam before he passed.

Within the next few years, you may be consulting with attorneys who never saw the inside of a law school because they took all of their courses on-line. Internet education is rapidly becoming the way of the future. Who knows whether this will produce greater legal abilities, or just enhanced computer skills.

Those who agree that not every lawyer is a "brain" may wonder how to determine the mental prowess of your future attorney. A wall full of framed documents is not always indicative of scholastic accomplishment. Some attorneys frame everything that has a seal. For example, membership in the American Bar Association is strictly voluntary. All the lawyer need do is sign up as a member, pay his annual dues and they will give him an impressive certificate of membership to hang on his wall. He might have framed a membership certificate from the local chamber of commerce. Again, all that is required is of him is to sign up and pay his dues.

If you get an opportunity, look at the framed documents and see what they represent. Two documents you will want to see are his law school degree and his license to practice. Hopefully, the law degree will be from a law school that you recognize. The state license will probably indicate that he is licensed to practice in any state court. If the lawyer practices in federal court, he should have a certificate stating that he is "duly admitted and qualified as an attorney and counselor of the District Court."

In your first visit, you may only be able to observe whether he has a lot of framed documents behind his desk or just a few. Do not give him a plus for lots of framed certificates, or a minus for few, unless you are able to read the documents and see what they represent.

EXPERIENCE

Closely related to knowledge is experience. Your lawyer may be straight out of law school with head crammed with all of the latest legal theories, but what they don't teach him in law school is how to *practice* law. This is much like having a doctor go through medical school and then letting him treat patients without going through an internship.

Most students realize that experience is an important part of their education. Once they pass the bar, they join an established law firm where their work is supervised. This is not to say that you should never employ a lawyer straight out of law school. The lawyer may have served an apprenticeship by working part-time with a law firm while he was attending law school, or he may have friends in the legal community who will guide him. But you need to ask about, and be aware of, his experience.

Not all fields of law require the services of a specialist, but he should have some experience in whatever legal problem you have. Later in this book we will explain when it is important to seek a specialist in a given field.

CERTIFICATION — AT LEAST HE'S COMPETENT

To be a "specialist" or "certified" means that the lawyer has practiced in a given field of law for a number of years (usually five) and has taken a test proving that he is knowledgable in that branch of law. He must keep his certification current by taking courses that keep him up to date with the law in that field.

In some states, the certification program is administered by the state Bar Association. In other states the Supreme Court of that state administers the program. Some states do not have a certification program, but they recognize certification programs offered by organizations such as the American Bar Association or the National Elder Law Foundation.

At the beginning of this chapter we said the qualities of Mr. Perfect Lawyer are knowledge, honesty, conscientiousness and loyalty to clients. You should have an opinion about his knowledge and experience within five minutes of your first meeting by listening to the way he speaks, examining the degrees he has accumulated and asking about his work experience. Honesty, conscientiousness and loyalty are not easily determined before you hire a lawyer, still you should keep these virtues in mind during your interview.

HONESTY

You expect your attorney to be honest in a monetary sense. If you give him a retainer (money for future work), you expect him to give you service in return. If you ask him to serve as escrow agent for the sale of your home, you expect that money to be there at closing. Attorneys who are not honest with client's funds are not lawyers for very long. They will quickly find themselves in criminal court and "de-barred," i.e., no longer able to practice law in the given state.

If you expect your attorney to place large sums of money in his trust or escrow account and you are concerned about the safety of those funds, before giving him the money, call the state Bar Association and ask whether he is licensed and in good standing. You can use your favorite search engine to locate the Bar Association in your state.

Honesty is more than a refusal to lie, steal or deceive. It is having integrity and living up to the basic legal principal of putting the client's interest ahead of his own. Honesty is difficult to determine at that first meeting and maybe not even after you get to know him better. You can't go by looks or personality. A good con artist can fool the most savvy of us. The best you can do is expect your attorney to be "up front" with you. Give him several minus points if you ever catch him in a lie. Better yet, find another lawyer.

CONSCIENTIOUSNESS

Conscientiousness is closely related to honesty. If your attorney says he will get a job done, does he complete it in a reasonable time? Does he keep you informed of the progress of the case?

Is he doing the job carefully, thoughtfully, or is he scrambling to get it to you at the last minute? Worse yet, have you heard him make excuses for missed deadlines?

Can you count on your lawyer to get the job done when he promises? If not, he is no Mr. Perfect Lawyer.

Again conscientiousness is one of those qualities that you may not pick up on during your first visit. But you can get some idea about whether he is conducting an orderly practice of law by looking around his office. Does he have boxes and files all over the place? Does he seem to not know where things are?

These are signs of an over-extended attorney. If you employ him, he may not be able to devote sufficient time to your problem. He may solve it, but it will be according to his time clock and not yours.

Another sign of an over-worked attorney (or maybe just one who is arrogant) is the attorney who puts layers of people between him and his client, in much the same manner as do doctors.

YOU CAN'T TALK TO GOD
(you might be able to talk to God's assistant), but
YOU CAN'T TALK TO GOD

Of late, doctors have taken to employing "physician assistants" to interface with the patients. The patient is greeted by a pleasant looking person, properly frocked with white medical coat and stethoscope. A new patients think they are talking to "*the* doctor" but that physician's assistant may have no more than a high school diploma, with some additional courses providing basic knowledge of medical terminology. Physician's assistants take blood pressure and draw blood for a battery of screening tests.

The person who goes in for an annual check-up may never see the doctor. If the result of the tests are within normal range, the patient may not even get to talk to him. The physician's assistant will call saying "Everything is fine. Just keep doing what-ever you're doing and we'll see you next year."

Unfortunately, many lawyers are following the doctor's lead. Some employ legal assistants to interact with the client whenever possible. You may be greeted by a legal assistant at your first meeting. The assistant will take basic information — name, address, telephone number, reason for the visit. Finally "*the* lawyer" comes in and you get to tell your story all over again. Give your new lawyer several minus points if you are subjected to this kind of treatment.

You may be greeted by the lawyer himself at your initial meeting, however he may keep you waiting for some time.

Give him a minus point for every minute he makes you wait. He has no respect for your time.

LOYALTY

Finally, we turn our attention to the most important quality of all, loyalty to the client. You might forgive your attorney for being pompous (i.e., full of himself) and sometimes late, but disloyalty to you is unforgivable.

Most clients do not even think about loyalty. After all the lawyer is being paid to represent the best interest of his client. Why should loyalty be an issue? You expect your lawyer to put your interests ahead of the opposing party, but will he put your interests ahead of his?

The client should always be aware of the ever present, *conflict of interest*. What is good for you may not be the best money-maker for the lawyer.

Simple example: you go to a lawyer for a Will expecting to pay a few hundred dollars. You walk away with a Trust costing thousands of dollars. Did you really need that Trust, or did your lawyer really need that income?

The client needs to be aware that a potential conflict of interest is involved in every attorney-client relationship .It is an invisible presence. Should it ever materialize and become an actual conflict of interest, then you have a problem.

In later chapters, we will deal with conflict of interest and explain how to defend yourself in the event your lawyer attempts to put his interests ahead of yours. We will also discuss what qualities are important for a lawyer in a given field of law. The personality of a Mr. Perfect Trial Lawyer is very different from the personality of Mr. Perfect Real Estate Lawyer. But their basic attributes should be the same. You want a lawyer who is knowledgeable, experienced in the field, honest, conscientious and loyal to you.

But where is Mr. Perfect?

It's well and good to know the qualities of a perfect attorney, but finding him is another matter. Perfection is an ideal and maybe doesn't even exist in the real world. A more realistic goal is to look for MR. RIGHT LAWYER.

Personal referral is usually the best method of finding Mr. Right. But make sure the lawyer practices in the field of law that you seek. If you want a divorce, you need a lawyer who does that for a living.

Your neighbor may have nothing but plaudits for the lawyer who got her a big settlement when she was hit by a car. But he is probably a Personal Injury attorney who knows nothing of Family Law.

If you know an attorney who did some work for you in the past, you might ask him whether he knows someone in the field you seek. Lawyers regularly refer clients back and forth to each other — for a price. Generally, it's 25% of the fee paid by the client. When asking your attorney for a referral you need to be thinking about a conflict of interest. Is he referring this lawyer because he will receive a fee? Will you be paying more to the other attorney to cover the cost of the referral?

Even without a referral fee, there could be other motives for the recommendation. Maybe that lawyer is someone who sends a lot of business to your lawyer and this is pay-back time. Maybe he is just your lawyer's drinking buddy.

You need to know more about the referral. You will want answers to the following questions:

Does your friend specialize in this type of law?

How long has he been practicing?

Will you be receiving a referral fee?

If you have no friend or attorney who can refer you to a lawyer who is experienced in the type of law you seek, call the state Bar Association. Most Bar Associations have referral programs. They can recommend an attorney who practices in your location. Lawyers who are on the referral list generally do not charge for the initial half hour consultation; however the referral service may ask the lawyer to collect a nominal fee from the client and then forward it as payment for the referral. You should be able to interview three different attorneys from the referral service for less than $100.

THREE ATTORNEYS???

People are strange. They will spend hours going from store to store looking for that perfect pair of shoes. The worse that can happen if you buy the wrong pair is that they hurt your feet and you take them back or pitch them out.

Employing MR. WRONG LAWYER can cost you a bundle, not only in money, but also emotionally. If you are not convinced that you need to take the time to find the right attorney for you, then read on. We promise you horror stories that should change your mind.

HOUSE BUYER BEWARE   2

Few people impulse buy a home; i.e., happen to see a house for sale, look at it and say "Yup, I'll take it." Most house purchases are carefully thought out, beginning with the financing. The buyer with a measure of common sense knows his first stop is to his friendly lender who will assist him in determining what he can afford. Next stop is the local real estate broker who will help him find the right home in that price range.

NEW OR USED?
If you are looking for a new home, you may want to shop on your own. New housing developments are widely advertised in newspapers and sometimes in local television ads. If you go shopping with a real estate broker, he may detour around new developments. Developers have their own sales force. The wise developer offers a commission to local real estate brokers, but that commission may be less than the broker can get from selling a home for a private owner.

The real estate broker makes the most money by selling his own listings; i.e., property which the owner has listed for sale with the broker under a Listing Contract. The commission promised to the broker is generally in the range of 5% to 10% of the selling price of the home — to be paid by the seller. If he sells a home listed by another broker, they share the commission, so he gets less for selling someone else's listing.

A potential conflict of interest is not unique to lawyers. It can occur with real estate brokers as well. Your real estate broker gets the greatest commission if he sells you his own listings. He may bypass more desirable properties in favor of his own listing. You should ask the broker whether he is the listing broker on any of the properties he intends to show you. If so, you need to ask to see properties listed by other brokers as well.

Buyer's Broker Or Seller's Broker?

There are "buyer's brokers" who have a contract with the buyer to find real property for purchase. This arrangement is common with wealthy and famous people. They can't shop for a home themselves so they employ someone to do so. It also occurs in the business world. A businessman may sign a contract agreeing to pay a commission to a real estate broker to locate suitable business property.

The person who shows you residential property is not a buyer's broker because you have not agreed to pay him if you purchase a home. He is the seller's broker because he is being paid by the seller to sell the property. This may not be a problem if he is trying to sell you property that another broker listed for sale. He can present your position to the listing broker and argue that the property should be sold for less than it's listed price. The listing agent can argue that it should be sold for list price.

A real estate broker who sells his own listing has no one to argue against. He must go directly to the seller and try to convince him to sell at the offered price.

This is a conflict of interest. The broker is being paid by the seller to get the highest price. You are not paying the broker to get the lowest price. The broker's commission is based on the selling price. The higher the price, the more money he makes. Expect the broker to try to get the best price for the seller.

Of course, the broker will say that he is just trying to get you both to market price so that you are both happy. And that is probably true because the broker gets nothing unless the house is sold. But how do you know if you are offering market price?

A real estate broker, who is a member of the local Board of Realtors®, has computer access to *comparables*. Comparables are properties in the same geographic area and with the same amenities as the property you are thinking of buying. He should be able to provide you with a computer print-out of comparable properties that were for sale during the past year, whether they were sold, and if so, the selling price.

By comparing the seller's asking price to past sales and to the asking price for other comparables on the market, you should be able to come up with the current market value of the property.

FOR SALE BY OWNER

You may have decided to buy a FSBO (pronounced "FIZBO"), an acronym for "For Sale By Owner." You may be thinking it is a good idea to buy a FSBO because there is no brokerage's fee involved. However, the reason the seller has not listed the property is because he does not want to pay a commission to a broker. He is not interested in giving you the benefit of those savings. He still wants his market price. Again, the question is how you determine market price.

Those with the time and ambition can check the newspapers and the Internet to see if there are any comparable sales. You can even go to the local recording department and find out how much the seller paid for the house, and when he bought it. Those with good social skills would do well to visit the neighborhood and ask neighbors whether the asking price is realistic.

Once you are ready to buy, the next thing to do is sign a contract. Who prepares the contract depends on local custom. In some states, such as New York, the attorney prepares a contract. In other states such as Florida, the real estate broker is allowed to help you complete a preprinted Sale and Purchase Agreement. If you are working with a Realtor®, he might offer you a contract prepared by the joint effort of the local board of Realtors® and attorneys from the state Bar Association. Such contracts are even handed, not favoring buyer or seller.

Some of the larger brokerage firms have their own "standard" form of sales contract. That contract may be fair as it relates to buyer and seller, but there may be provisions in the contract that favor the brokerage firm. The contract may contain wording that protects the brokerage firm from a law suit. It may include a special fee to be paid either by buyer or seller to the brokerage firm. Some of the larger brokerage firms have their own title insurance company, and will want to steer business to that company. The brokerage firm contract may provide that their title company will do the closing.

A person who is selling his own home may have a sales contract that he received as part of a sales package he purchased to assist him in selling his property.

A developer of a planned residential community usually offers a package of materials that includes a floor plan of the home to be purchased, homeowner's association documents, and a sales contract.

In all of these cases, you can take a copy of the sales contract but don't sign it unless you know what you are signing. Not signing a sales contract until her lawyer explained it to her was the one right thing that Denise did when she bought her first house.

Denise never thought of herself as a career woman. She had a good-paying job as a computer technician, but she hardly considered that to be a "career." She thought of herself as just a working girl who would eventually marry and settle down.

When she turned 40 she realized her self-image needed a reality check.

She told her friend Angie, "Young girls should not be allowed to see Disney cartoon films — you know the ones that have the princess kissing the toad and turning it into a prince, and then riding off to live happily ever after. That gives young girls the wrong impression. They see the film and expect to marry Prince Charming. Every prince I ever kissed turned into a toad."

"What brought all this on?"

"Here I am forty years old and what do I have to show for it? The same job, the same apartment, the same old, same old, for over ten years. I always expected I would live in a house with a white picket fence and have beautiful, happy children playing in the yard. "

"Well, I don't know about Prince Charming and his offspring, but you make a good salary. There's no reason you can't have that house with the white picket fence."

Denise felt as if a light had turned on. Why not buy her own home?

She prevailed on Angie to help her find the perfect home. It didn't take too long. There was a new development going up in the area. The salesperson showed her a home that was nearing completion. Denise loved the floor plan. But the thing that sold her was its beautiful lake view. She was ready to sign on the dotted line when Angie said, under her breath, "Buy in haste — repent at leisure."

Denise asked "What's that mean?"

"Ever hear of Buyer's Remorse? That's when some-one moves too quickly and buys a house before thinking the whole thing through."

The sales person moved to close the deal. "Listen, these houses are really selling. You have a prime lot here. I can't promise to hold it for you. My next customer might buy the house out from under you. If you want the house, you need to give me a deposit and sign this contract now."

Denise looked at the contract. It was four pages long and written in small print. She didn't know if she understood what all of those paragraphs meant, but she really wanted the house.

Angie came to the rescue. "Denise needs to have her lawyer review this contract and the homeowner association documents before she can close the deal. She can sign the contract and give you a deposit, but you need to add a paragraph that says 'This contract is subject to the review of the buyer's attorney. All monies shall be returned to the buyer in the event her attorney does not approve the contract within three business days.'"

The salesperson said she would need to consult with her manager before making any change to the contract. Not surprisingly, he agreed to allow three days for the review of the contract.

Denise had to scramble to find a real estate lawyer. None of her friends knew one they could recommend, so she looked in the telephone book under ATTORNEYS, REAL ESTATE and called one whose office was close to where she worked.

The lawyer's secretary said she couldn't speak to the attorney because he was with a client, however the secretary assured her that he was an experienced Real Estate attorney. She said the initial consultation would be $200. Denise thought that was high, but she didn't have time to shop around for a lawyer. She made an appointment for the next day.

The lawyer was almost twenty minutes late, but he apologized and was otherwise very nice.

He said he had several closings with this developer. "This contract was drafted by the developer's attorney, for the benefit of the developer. Notice there is no firm closing date. The contract says, in effect, that closing will take place within sixty days, but if the house isn't finished, it will be closed whenever it is."

They went over the rest of the contract. Denise was surprised with how one-sided the contract was, all in the favor of the developer. The contract required that the closing take place at the title insurance company named in the contract. Her lawyer explained, "The developer owns that title insurance company. This contract requires that you pay all of the closing costs, including your title insurance policy. He's even having you reimburse him for taxes he paid for the year."

"That doesn't seem fair. We may not close until September. Why should I pay taxes for the whole year?"

"This contract is designed to give the developer extra income at closing. Your closing costs will probably run $5,000 and he will get a good chunk of that money. He could have increased the price of the house a few thousand dollars. Instead he gets the price he wanted in the form of closing fees."

That was an eye-opener for Denise. But she wanted the house. Her lawyer assured her that the developer had been doing business in the area for a long time and stood behind his product, so she decided to go through with the purchase.

The attorney asked whether she wanted him to represent her at closing. Denise felt that there was a lot she didn't know about this house-buying game so she signed a retainer agreement agreeing to pay him $200 an hour (plus costs) to represent her in the purchase of this home.

She kept in touch with her lawyer over the next few months. Finally, they had a closing date. She went to his office to go over the closing statement.

She was surprised to see her attorney's fee placed on the closing statement to be paid at closing. It was over $2,000. Her attorney gave her his record of time and costs. She didn't realize that he had been charging to the nearest quarter hour. He charged $50 whenever she called, even if they spoke only for a few minutes.

His billing statement did show that he spent considerable time reviewing the homeowner's association documents, the proposed deed, title insurance policy, the survey of the property and other documents related to the closing, so she felt that most of his fee was for work done.

He explained that his fees would be paid to him at closing and he would meet her at the title company at that time.

Closing took longer than expected — mostly because of the mortgage. The bank sent the closing package to the closing agent at the last minute, so her lawyer had to take the time at closing to review the loan documents. Finally, all the documents were signed and she was given the keys to the house. The lawyer said he would mail her the original recorded deed and title insurance policy just as soon as he received them from the title company.

Two months later, she received the deed, title insurance policy and another bill for over $1,000. He charged for time spent at closing, his travel time to and from closing and the time he took to look over the deed and title insurance policy. He even charged her for the time he took to write the final billing letter to her.

His costs were equally as comprehensive. He charged for copies, telephone calls, postage, fax sent and received and $1 a mile as travel costs to and from the closing!

If she knew he was going to charge for mileage, she would have picked a lawyer who had an office in the same town as the closing.

She called to complain about the bill "I thought you were paid at closing."

He explained "If you look at the billing statement I gave you during your last office visit, you will see that it was current up to that day. You agreed to pay me $200 an hour. This bill is for the work I did after that date."

Denise paid the bill, but she vowed never to use that lawyer again or to ever sign an open-ended retainer agreement.

House Seller Beware

Some years later Denise was offered an excellent job in another state. She decided to take the job and sell her home. This time she shopped around to find an attorney who would assist her with the sale. She settled on an attorney who owned his own title insurance company.

The reader is probably thinking "Conflict of interest." But it is only a potential conflict of interest. As you will see, it could work out in the client's favor.

Denise was very sure to get a clear understanding of fees before she employed the attorney. She explained how unhappy she was with the attorney who represented her when she bought the house.

He said "I will charge $200 an hour to review any contract submitted to you by the buyer. If you wish, I will draft the contract for the buyer to sign."

"Wouldn't drafting a contract take a lot of time? The last one I signed was four pages long."

"Not in this age of technology. My contracts are on computer. All I have to do is fill in information specific to this closing such as name, addresses, legal description, closing date, etc. I will not charge more than $200 to draft the contract."

"What about closing?"

"If the buyer agrees to close with my title insurance company, I will not charge to represent you at closing. The amount I charge for the title insurance policy and closing costs is sufficient compensation — assuming we do not have any unusual problem."

"What kind of problem?"

"If for some reason, you do not have clear title to your home and I need to do work to clear title, I will charge you for that work."

"I don't see how that could be a problem. I was the first owner of the house."

"Good title depends on the land under the house. When examining title we need to be sure that the person who sold you the house had the right to sell the land under it to you."

"But I bought it from the developer; and I paid for title insurance, so if there is a problem, at least I'm insured."

The attorney agreed that there shouldn't be a problem. He told her to call when she found a buyer for her home.

As it turned out, the buyer had much the same deal with his attorney as was offered to Denise. The buyer offered her a contract prepared by his lawyer that required the buyer's lawyer to do the closing.

The buyer explained, "My attorney is an agent for a title insurance company. He will issue my title policy and do the closing. He has agreed not to charge me additional attorney fees for the closing."

Denise had her lawyer review the contract before she signed it. He said "This looks fine. It's one of those standard contracts used in the area. It is designed to be fair to both buyer and seller. You'll be closing next month. I don't see any need for me to be with you at closing. I can review your closing statement and any closing document they want you to sign before the closing. I will make myself available by telephone during your closing. You can call me if a problem comes up. "

"How much time do you expect to spend reviewing the closing documents?"

"I know how you feel about open-ended fee agreements. I'll charge a flat fee of $500 to be paid at closing. That fee includes my review of the sales contract and the closing documents. It also includes any telephone calls to me before, during or after closing. If for some reason we run into a problem and I need to spend more than three hours on this case, we will discuss a new fee agreement."

As it was, the closing went smoothly. Denise was sure she had found Mr. Right Real Estate Lawyer. The only problem was that Denise was moving to another state, so she would need to find another Mr. Right Lawyer to help her buy a home in that state.

How To Defend Yourself
Against Your Real Estate Lawyer

After reading the tale of Denise, you probably have a good idea of what not to do when you're buying a house. Her first mistake was to get herself in a bind so that she was pressured into hiring the first lawyer she met.

Your best defense is to line up Mr. Right Real Estate Attorney before you go house hunting.

EXPERIENCE

When looking for a Real Estate attorney, you will want one who is experienced in examining title to real estate. Those who are qualified to write a title insurance policy are knowledgable in the field. In addition, they have access to lawyers in the title insurance company who can answer questions that may arise with respect to whether the property you are buying has good title.

Title insurance is not the common practice in all states. In many states the attorney prepares an Abstract of Title giving a condensed history of the recorded documents that affect the property. The Abstract will show whether the seller has clear title to the property; i.e., has the right to sell it to you. Whichever is the practice in your state you will want to know about your attorney's background in real property. Has he taken special courses in title examination? What percentage of his practice is devoted to real estate?

THE OPEN-ENDED FEE AGREEMENT

The second mistake Denise made when buying the house was to sign an open-ended retainer agreement; i.e., one with no maximum limit on fees. If your lawyer insists on charging by the hour, have him give you an estimate of the time he will spend. An experienced attorney knows how many hours he usually spends on a closing. If he will not give you an estimate of his time or if his estimated fee is more than you can afford, look for another lawyer.

If the hourly fee seems reasonable, try to "hem in" the cost of the job. Try to negotiate a flat fee, with a maximum number of hours the attorney will spend to earn that fee. That was the arrangement Denise had with her lawyer when she was selling her home.

Make sure your fee agreement specifies whether you will be charged to the nearest tenth or nearest quarter hour. A tenth of an hour is six minutes (.1 X 60 = 6 min.). A quarter of an hour is fifteen minutes. Naturally, you will insist on 6 minute billing increments.

THE OPEN-ENDED COST AGREEMENT

Costs is another thing that needs to be spelled out. Your best position is to have your retainer agreement state that there will be no charge for costs. If your agreement makes no mention of costs, or says "plus costs," you need to know what costs are involved and how much will be charged for each item.

Have your retainer agreement state what will be charged for long-distance calls, fax charge per page, postage per letter, express mail charges, legal research fees, travel expenses, and any other out-of-pocket expense usually associated with the representation of a house buyer.

THE FIXED PRICE AGREEMENT

Attorneys who are qualified to write title insurance policies often include their attorney's fees as part of the cost of the title insurance policy. In many states, the Department of Insurance regulates title insurance premiums. Those states have a *promulgated* (published) title insurance rate table. The table gives the lowest amount a title insurance company can charge for a title insurance policy based on the value of the home.

If your attorney agrees to do the closing for just the cost of title insurance policy, you need to ask whether the amount he will charge for title insurance is the lowest rate allowed under state law. If not, you need to ask how much more is being charged to you above that rate. It may be that the amount above the lowest promulgated rate is equal to an amount he would have charged to represent you at closing.

Give the lawyer a minus for honesty if he says he is not charging for attorney fees, but the flat fee charged is significantly more than the promulgated rate. Better yet, find an attorney who will do the closing for the lowest promulgated rate.

DIY (Do It Yourself)　3
Who Needs Lawyers Anyway?

ACT IV, Scene 2, line 86 of the second part of
Shakespeare's Henry VI is often misquoted and
misunderstood. Line 86 says "The first thing we do,
let's kill all the lawyers." In the play, this sentence
was spoken by an anarchist who was trying to over-
throw the government of England. He said it, not
because he hated all lawyers, but because he knew
the lawyers were committed to upholding the law.
He wanted to kill the lawyers to eliminate those who
understood and would defend the laws of England.
So the line is not anti-lawyer but pro-lawyer.

People may have a similar misconception about
this book. The title may lead people to think that the
book is anti-lawyer. It isn't. Lawyers are necessary
to our society. It is the lawyer who brought about
social change by suing manufacturers of unsafe
cars, unsafe drugs and unsafe products such as
tobacco. Where would the American public be if
lawyers didn't hit big business where they hurt,
namely in their pocket?

Lawyers are needed even more so today to advocate the rights of the people. The message of this
book is not to do away with lawyers, but to keep
them honest. Too many lawyers behave like the
Mr. Wrongs described in this book.

Lawyers have a built-in advantage — not because they are smarter than the client, but because they know how the game is played. The "game" being our legal system of justice. The reader can defend himself against being taken by Mr. Wrong Lawyer by making himself aware of what legal advice he needs to "buy" and then demanding that advice at a reasonable price.

The person with limited assets may be wondering why he needs to bother with a lawyer in the first place. But the need to seek legal advise is much like the need to consult with a doctor. There are lots of over-the-counter drugs, but if you take seriously ill, you need a doctor. Similarly, there are legal things you can do yourself, but if you have a serious legal problem, you need a lawyer.

We will be discussing when you can take that legal aspirin, and when you need a "prescription" from your lawyer. Buying a house is one of those lawyer moments.

BUYING A HOUSE

Buying a house is not the time to DIY unless you are an experienced real estate broker, or you are working as a legal assistant in a law firm that specializes in real property law — and even then you should have your boss look over your contract. For most of us, buying a home is the single largest purchase we will ever make. Trying to save money on legal fees could cost you a bundle later on. You need a lawyer to protect you and your investment.

THE CONTRACT

You need a Real Estate lawyer to prepare or review your sales contract. He should explain what each paragraph means. Some sentences that appear in sales contracts are deceptively simple. "Time is of the essence" is one of them.

You may think that this sentence is saying that time is important. And you'd be right. But the legal effect of that sentence is "You will be in breach of this contract, if you don't meet its deadlines." In other words, if you are late with making a payment or if you don't show up for closing as scheduled, you could be sued.

EXAMINE TITLE

You need a Real Estate lawyer to examine title to the property to be sure that the seller has the right to transfer the property to you.

Some may think that they can purchase title insurance and that will protect them. They believe the title company won't issue a policy unless title to the property is clear. This is not necessarily true. Each title insurance policy contains a list of EXCEPTIONS. An Exception is something that is not covered in your policy. The title insurance company will try to include as many Exceptions as possible. Mr. Right Real Estate Lawyer will demand that there be as few Exceptions as possible. After he finishes negotiating with the title insurance company, he should explain to you what Exceptions remain in your policy and what risks are associated with each Exception.

You also need to keep in mind that title insurance is limited to the face value of your policy. Home values can double or triple over a relatively short period of time. If you do not have an attorney to challenge each Exception and a problem later appears, the most you will receive from the title insurance company is the amount you paid for the house.

THE SURVEY

A survey will reveal the boundaries of the property and whether anyone is encroaching (intruding) on your property. For example, a survey should reveal whether the neighbor's fence is over the boundary line onto the property you are buying. If it is, your lawyer will inform the seller that he needs to have that fence moved before you go to closing. If you close without a survey, that fence is going to be your problem and not the seller's problem.

THE CLOSING STATEMENT

The closing statement is a listing of the credits and debits to the buyer and to the seller. It's your lawyer's job to see to it that you are not charged for items that should be paid for by the seller. Once he is satisfied that the statement is correct, he should go over the closing statement with you, line by line.

BE THERE FOR YOU

I spent many years as a Real Estate lawyer. It was surprising how many problems popped up between the signing of the contract and the closing. The closing itself was generally a stressful time. Buyers worry about whether they paid too much for the house. Some worry about whether they will be able to keep up their house payments. Sellers are concerned about moving to a new location. It's a transition time for both buyer and seller, and transitions are difficult.

A harmonious purchase and sale was the exception, not the rule. It is important to have a lawyer on your side who will tell the seller, or the seller's attorney, when he is out of line.

SELLING A HOUSE

Selling a house is different from buying a house. As a seller, it's take your money and run. Yet there are still reasons you might want to employ a lawyer.

THE SALES CONTRACT

You may have learned enough about sales contracts when you purchased your home to be able to read and understand the contract presented by the buyer. If you have a real estate broker, he should be able to explain any part of the offer that is not clear to you. If you are selling your home without the assistance of a real estate broker, and the buyer asks that you provide the contract, you may need to employ an attorney to prepare the contract.

THE CLOSING

You may live in a state where it is the practice to close with a title insurance company. It could be that neither you or the buyer has a lawyer and you decide to close with a title company. You may think you both are on even footing, but that may not be the case. Whoever is paying for title insurance may have worked a deal with the title company to charge as much as possible to the other party.

Usually the buyer pays for title insurance. If he employs the title company and you are charged more than you think fair, no one will be in your corner to speak on your behalf.

People who close at a title company without the assistance of a lawyer also need to be aware that while the title company does not represent buyer or seller, it does represent itself. Each title insurance company has its lawyer prepare forms to be signed by buyer and seller at closing. Those forms are designed to protect the title company. The lawyer may prepare forms that limit the right of the buyer and seller to hold the title company responsible for any mistake they make. You will want to resist signing any form prepared by the title company that says you will "... hold harmless and indemnify ..." the company from any loss. By signing such a document you are promising to reimburse the title company for losses they may suffer as a result of the closing, even if that loss was caused by something they did!

BE THERE FOR YOU

If you have Mr. Right with you at closing, he will not allow you to sign documents that can only benefit the title company. He will restrict the documents you sign to just those required by your sales contract.

He will also be on your side if the buyer acts unreasonably. I recall one closing in which a couple was purchasing a condominium. The husband was irritable and finding fault with everything. My patience was strained when he said, "Who is going to clean the closet?"

I didn't know what he was talking about. My client moved out the previous week and left the apartment in good condition.

"What closet?" I asked.

"The hall closet. The rack to hang clothes is not clean. It needs to be washed down. So who is going to clean the closet?"

I explained to him that the contract he signed required the apartment be empty and cleanly swept and it was more than that.

"I'm not moving into that pig stye."

I wish I could say that I won him over with my keen legal reasoning or with my wit and charm. But, no. I glared at him and was about to have some sharp words about breach of contract, when his wife put her hand on his arm.

It was one of those gestures that married couples make to each other. A silent communication. She took a pen and began signing the closing documents. He followed her lead without another word.

At the end we all smiled and shook hands.

I wished them the very best with their new home.

So You Want A Divorce $$$??   4

Divorce can be a rough time for family — not just the husband, wife and children but for the rest of the family. Grandparents are often profoundly affected and disturbed by the break-up. The stress associated with a divorce is usually intense. Those seeking divorce may not be thinking clearly and may be behaving badly. The person seeking a divorce, and / or his spouse, may be angry, anxious, greedy, selfish, demanding and irrational.

The saying in legal circles is that criminal attorneys see bad people at their best behavior. Divorce attorneys see good people at their worst behavior.

The transition from married to single is an all encompassing experience. The person going through the process needs to recognize that they may have too much on their mind to be fully aware of all that is going on. This is the time to make a sincere effort to find Mr. Right Lawyer. At the end of this chapter we will describe the qualities to seek.

The person going through a divorce also needs to be aware that there are pitfalls in the *Family Law*** procedure itself. The story you are about to read shows how a person seeking a divorce may find himself fighting the judicial system as well as his spouse.

** In some states, it is called *Domestic Law*.

Many people who seek a divorce are unaware that the judge may be working against them. But the lawyers do.

That was the case with Robert. He was a personable guy with natural sex appeal. He wasn't a particularly good lawyer. His legal arguments were sloppy. His research skills, non-existent. Still, with his winning personality and the assistance of a sharp legal assistant, he became a successful divorce attorney.

Robert was good friends with those in the legal community, from court stenographers, to the county clerk. Even other lawyers who opposed him on a regular basis, liked him. He would socialize with lawyers and judges at Bar functions, and for those in his financial bracket, at his country club.

Because of his advanced social skills there were few times Robert didn't get his way. People just wanted to please him. For example, the county clerk would always assign Robert's cases to a good judge, i.e., one who is impartial and who made his ruling based on the law.

It's an advantage to have a good judge. Lawyers know they will get a fair hearing and a just ruling. Lawyers try to avoid having their case heard by a bad judge; i.e., one who rules on whim, not logic, and not necessarily on the law.

The clerk of the court is supposed to assign cases to a judge on a rotating basis. But that's not how it works in many court systems. Clerks assign a good judge to their favorite lawyers. And that was certainly the case with Robert. The only time he went before a bad judge was when the opposing counsel filed the case and had the misfortune to be assigned to that judge.

Robert continued his comfortable and lucrative, practice for over twenty years. He approached middle age with a somewhat expanded waistline, but he maintained his natural sex appeal.

A new judge was appointed to the bench. Esther was thin, dark haired and ten years Robert's senior. They met at a Bar luncheon. As was his practice with all new judges, he made it his business to sit next to her to get to know her. Robert sensed that Esther was a hungry person. Not for the food that she picked at on her plate, but for affection and approval. He knew that kind of hunger could never be satisfied. He decided to use that yearning to his advantage. He did charitable work in the community and invited her to participate in the next fund raising activity. She readily agreed.

He thought "This is going to be too easy."

And it was. They soon became fast friends.

Esther never presided over a case handled by her lawyer husband. If her husband was ever assigned to her court, she would immediately recuse (remove) herself from the case. Yet she deluded herself into thinking that she was impartial whenever Robert appeared before her. He knew differently.

This was a flirtation with disaster. Should they act on their impulse and be discovered, their respective marriages could be destroyed. Worse than the loss of a marriage for two such ambitious people, would be the loss of their license to practice law. Having an affair with a judge who regularly presides over the lawyer is a conflict of interest. To be discovered would destroy both careers.

The flirtation could have gone on indefinitely, but Robert lusted for Esther. Was it love or just the excitement of a dangerous liaison? Maybe it was just the ultimate power orgasm of a lawyer being in bed with a judge, literally.

They were very careful about when and where they met. Yet there was no denying that she was sixteen-year-old-first-crush-smitten. She took to flirting with other lawyers in open court as a cover for her feelings for Robert. Smiling coyly, batting her eye-lashes, brushing her hair back to reveal her neck — but she fooled no one. There were whispers around the courthouse. Lawyers from neighboring counties began to refer to this court as Peyton Place.

Robert was such a popular guy that no one wanted to get involved in an expose'. Besides, you would need to catch them red-faced in the act and they were discrete enough not to let that happen.

Still, some lawyers bristled. There are many times before going to trial that lawyers go to court to argue some procedural matter or point of law. It soon became apparent that there was no point in arguing these minor skirmishes before Esther and against Robert. They would lose every time. The lawyers began to either work out the problem with Robert out of court or simply let him have his way.

Robert, being good buddies with his fellow lawyers would try, whenever possible, to work out a mutually agreeable solution.

That was until Barbara happened on the scene. She was just out of law school — chuck full of legal theories and respect for the law. She had a law suit with Robert as opposing attorney. She didn't know how the game was played, so she scheduled a deposition of Robert's client at her office, some thirty miles away from Robert's office.

Robert's secretary called Barbara saying she needed to take the deposition at his office and at his convenience, otherwise Robert would file a Motion for a Protective Order to stop Barbara from taking the deposition. Barbara snapped back "Let him do just that."

Barbara thought the threat of a Protective Order was just to intimidate her. She couldn't imagine Robert filing such a motion. According to the law, a Protective Order was proper only if the deposition was being taken to harass the witness or if there was some valid reason that the witness could not appear, such as illness or disability. None of these applied in this case. All Robert objected to was the time and place of the deposition. He must surely be bluffing. He wasn't.

Robert filed his Motion for Protective Order and set it for the Motion Calendar before judge Esther. A Motion Calendar hearing is a hearing before the judge to take care of small matters. Judges usually set aside an hour in the morning to hear such motions. Each attorney gets a few minutes to present his argument. The other attorneys sit around listening to the arguments until it is their turn to present their own Motion to the judge. There were about twenty lawyers present at the Motion Calendar hearing that morning.

Barbara was surprised to see that Robert had ordered a court reporter for the hearing. Usually a court reporter is called in for important matters in which you want to contest the judge's ruling. Little did Barbara know that this was strictly for the benefit of letting her believe that there was a possibility that the judge would not rule in his favor.

Hardly likely with the relationship between Robert and Esther.

Robert presented his argument to the judge. Barbara was fully prepared and gave a statement of the law and the rules of court that clearly favored her position. The judge ignored her argument and said "I think there is some sort of court rule saying that if the parties cannot agree upon a place for the deposition to be heard, it must be held in the court-house."

Barbara's heart sunk. Robert's office was less than a mile from the courthouse. If there was such a rule, she would lose this battle. Esther looked into her rule book to try to find that rule, but she was unable to find it. She gave the book to Robert saying "Here, you find the rule while I hear some of these other motions."

Robert took the book and asked Barbara to join him outside of the courtroom to try to locate the rule. Once outside, they negotiated the setting of the deposition. He would have his client go to Barbara's office for the deposition provided she rescheduled it at a time convenient to him.

They went back into the courtroom and Robert said "Judge, we couldn't find the rule, but we agreed that the deposition will be held at the scheduled place, but at a different time."

Thinking that Robert had lost the argument, Esther flew off the handle "I am not going to allow a deposition to be held at a dangerous location."

Barbara wondered what the heck was going on. Robert had not raised any issue about the safety of the location. Where was this judge coming from?

Robert said "No, it's O.K. Judge. We worked this out."

But Esther continued to carry on, threatening to grant his motion.

Robert said "No, it's O.K., Really. It's O.K, Really, Really. We worked it out, really."

Robert used a tone reserved for a husband who is trying to quiet an out of control wife. Like a dutiful wife, Esther finally settled down and agreed to the arrangement.

All the other attorneys in the room put their eyes down. They didn't want to see or hear this argument.

Barbara looked at Esther and Robert and knew exactly what was going on. She had heard that Robert and Esther had a special relationship, but she thought people were referring to the fact that they both worked on charitable projects together. This "special relationship" had nothing to do with charity.

Barbara was appalled. She fully intended to blow the whistle on this most corrupt court.

All she needed to do was get hold of the court reporter's transcript of the hearing and present it to the Chief Judge. She called the court reporter's office and ordered the transcript. Weeks passed and no transcript. She called the owner of the court reporter service. He said he didn't know the reason for the delay, but he would get right on it.

Two more weeks passed and still no transcript. More calls to the owner. Finally she received the transcript, but it was doctored. There was no "It's O.K., Really. It's O.K. Really, Really. We worked it out, really."

In its place was "We appreciate the court's concern, but we have come to a mutually agreeable solution and we thank the court for its attention to this matter."

Obviously this court reporter had a long standing relationship with Robert. Either Robert used his considerable charm to convince her to change what was said, or maybe she was afraid that not to do so would mean he would blackball her company and hurt business. Maybe both.

Barbara was not going to give up. She called the state licensing agency to take the court reporter up on charges. But she was in for a rude awakening. Her state did not license court reporters. Anyone could be a court reporter. They answer to no one. And that state is not unique. Many states have no licensing requirements for court reporters.

This particular skirmish between Barbara and Robert did not hurt Barbara's case. It only related to the time and place the deposition would be held. However, Barbara knew the score. There was no way her client could come out ahead in a court battle with Esther as the judge.

There was nothing Barbara could do about it. She couldn't even explain the problem to her client. If she did, and it got back to Robert or Esther, without hard evidence, Barbara could be sued for slander. She thought about withdrawing from the case, but another lawyer would have no better chance. You can beat an opposing counsel, but you cannot beat a crooked judge.

Barbara decided to try to settle the case in mediation.

Robert knew he was in a position of power. He advised his client not to settle for less than he wanted. At mediation, Robert said that their offer was fair and firm. He said that they were prepared to go to trial if the wife didn't agree to the proposed terms. He confidently said that the wife would not do any better if they went to trial. In fact, she would probably do a lot worse.

Barbara met privately with her client and said she agreed with Robert "We can go to trial, but chances are that the judge will not award you more than what you husband is now offering. It's better to settle now and save the cost of going to trial."

The wife accepted the settlement, but she walked away with much less than she should have.

The reader is probably thinking, "Interesting story, but that only happens on television (and in this author's imagination)."

Not so. It doesn't happen very often. But it does happen. Judges do have sexual relationships with lawyers. More commonly, however, the abuse is one of favoritism. Judges play favorites for any number of reasons. Judges are just like the general population. They have their hang-ups and prejudices. And there may be monetary reasons. We have all read of cases where a judge was found guilty of accepting bribes.

For those states that elect judges there is legal bribery. Attorneys contribute considerable funds to the campaign to elect the judge.

For those states whose judges are appoint through government appointment, politics may play an important role in a judge's decision. See an excellent discussion by Alan M. Dershowitz, in his book *Supreme Injustice,* of how politics influenced the decision of the Supreme Court in the case of <u>Bush v. Gore</u>.

You may find that you need to defend yourself against your attorney and the judicial system itself.

How To Defend Yourself Against
Your Divorce Lawyer

He didn't know it, but the husband who employed Robert didn't need to protect himself against the judicial system. He just knew that Robert had a reputation of being a very successful lawyer. His high attorney fees and fancy offices were proof enough that Robert knew his way around the courthouse. Barbara's client made the mistake of employing a lawyer fresh out of law school. In Family Law, experience counts a lot.

The wife might have thought that she couldn't afford an expensive attorney, but in every state, the court has the power to level the playing field by ordering the partner with lots of money to pay for the legal representation of the partner with little or no money. The wife's attorney could have asked the court to order the husband to pay for his wife's representation. With the husband paying for his lawyer, and his wife's lawyer, he might not have been so willing to go to trial.

Not all divorces involve high stakes demanding the services of a high-powered divorce attorney. The average person can be well represented by a competent divorce lawyer at a reasonable fee. When employing a divorce lawyer, there are things the client needs to be aware of and defend against.

EXPERIENCE

You will want to seek the services of an attorney who specializes in Family Law. If your state has a certification program for Family Law, employ a lawyer who is so certified. Your attorney may proudly announce to you that he is a Certified Trial Lawyer. That is not necessarily a plus. True, if you need to go to trial, you want someone who is experienced. But going to trial is expensive monetarily and emotionally. You want an attorney who will go to trial only as a last resort. A litigator may be too willing to go to trial. If you employ someone who is a trial attorney, make it clear to him that you intend to explore all avenues of settlement before you decide to go to trial.

LOYALTY

Does your lawyer really believe in your case? Your attorney may not be sympathetic with your cause but, like most of us, he needs to pay the rent and will take jobs that he is less than enthusiastic about. You might be able to pick up on his feelings about your case in the first meeting. Does he seem genuinely concerned about your plight, or is he busy explaining the argument that your spouse will probably use against you?

If he seems non-committal, ask him whether he is active in any advocacy organization. There are organizations such as NOW (the National Organization For Women) that advocate women's rights.

Other organizations are active in the rights of a father to have custody of his child. Divorce attorneys often join an advocacy group as a means of "rainmaking" (lawyer talk for drumming up business). They usually join organizations with which they are most in tune philosophically.

Knowing what groups he belongs to will give you an idea as to whether he is a men's rights lawyer or a women's rights lawyer. Naturally you will seek a lawyer who is inclined to your position. A man trying to get custody of his child, may not be well served by a feminist attorney who is a member of a mother's rights group.

AVAILABILITY

Messy marriages lead to messy divorces. By messy we mean a marriage that is plagued with abuse, emotional and physical, or one involving addiction to something — booze, drugs, gambling, sex. Such unions are volatile and can erupt into a crisis situation at any given time not just 9 to 5, Monday to Friday. More likely than not, that emergency situation will happen on the weekend or after hours. Even with a restraining order issued by the court, a partner might show up after hours. Police may need to be called. The client may need to have his lawyer bail him out of jail.

Those who expect a messy divorce need to employ an attorney who is prepared to come to his client's aid at any time day or night. Even those who anticipate an amicable separation should ask "How can I reach you if there is some sort of after hour emergency."

Give the lawyer a plus, plus, plus, who says "Here's my cell phone number."

Give the lawyer a plus, plus, who says "I'm not usually available after hours, but I have an answering service who can reach me in case of emergency."

Give the lawyer a plus who says "My answering service can reach me, or my partner, if there's an emergency. "

You know what to give the lawyer who makes no provision for after-hours emergencies.

CONFLICT OF INTEREST

Divorce attorneys work by the hour. The more they work, the more they get paid. It is in your best interest to get the divorce behind you as quickly as possible, but without jeopardizing your financial position. To make sure that this potential conflict of interest does not become an actual conflict of interest, you need to come to an agreement before you employ an attorney regarding time and cost.

In your first meeting have your attorney explain the laws of your state and the customary family law practice in your county. Many states have guidelines regarding child support and alimony. By learning about the law and customary outcomes in your state, you can develop realistic expectations. You also need to have your attorney give you some concept of how much time it will take to get your divorce.

THE RETAINER AGREEMENT

All the things we said about the retainer agreement in Chapter 2 apply here. Usually the client comes out best with a fixed price agreement. More likely your lawyer will want an open-ended retainer agreement with no limit on fees or costs.

But all things in life are negotiable. An experienced attorney should know how much time he will spend at each stage of the divorce proceeding. He should be able to set a realistic price based on his estimated time. Try to get your lawyer to agree to an upper limit on costs and a fee agreement based on different stages of the case.

THE STAGED FEE AGREEMENT

A Staged Fee Agreement is one in which payment is based on different stages of representation. The retainer agreement sets an upper limit for each stage. For example, a divorce lawyer might require payment at four stages of the representation

1. THE INITIAL FILING

Your lawyer needs to file the law suit and have your spouse served with the complaint. If your spouse has already filed for divorce, your lawyer will need to prepare and file an answer to the complaint.

2. THE DISCOVERY PROCESS

Your attorney will need to discover as much evidence as possible to support your case, and as much damaging evidence as he can, to hurt the case of your spouse.

3. MEDIATION

Most states require the parties to attend mediation to try to resolve their differences. Your attorney will need to prepare for the mediation by compiling all of the evidence favorable to your case. If the mediation is successful, he will prepare a settlement agreement for you and your spouse to sign.

4. THE TRIAL

You may never get to stage 4 because you and your spouse have been able to settle your differences by agreement. Any dead-locked issue will need to be decided by a judge at trial.

How To Defend Against
The Judicial System

Most divorce cases are decided by a judge and not a jury, so it is important that the judge in your case be fair and impartial. If your attorney is on good terms with the clerk who assigns cases to a judge, it may be to your advantage to have your lawyer file the lawsuit.

Once your case is assigned to a judge, you need to ask your attorney about that judge. Hopefully, he will say good things. If not, you may have a problem. If your lawyer complains that the judge is a "loose cannon," it means that there is no predicting how he will rule.

That may not necessarily be a bad thing. If the other side also sees the judge as being unpredictable, they (and you) should be motivated to settle the matter without going to trial.

If your lawyer complains that the judge is biased and is not going to be inclined to see things your way, you may find yourself in the position of being forced to settle for less. Rather than accept this helpless position, consider fighting the system. In many states, Court Watch groups have been formed. Volunteers attend trials of certain judges to observe their courtroom behavior.

In Florida, Families Against Court Travesties (" FACTS") is one such group. Sometimes just a court appearance by FACTS is enough to change the way a judge conducts himself.

You can get more information about Court Watch groups from the Internet. You can use the National Organization for Women (NOW) as a starting point for your search.

We will be discussing other ways that you can work to improve the judicial system in the last chapter of this book.

THE DIY DIVORCE

Those who marry have a 50-50 chance that they will eventually divorce. With odds like that you wonder why anyone would take the risk. No doubt those who marry think they are going to be in the "till death do us part" half; but 50% of them will be wrong and find themselves trying to figure out the fastest and cheapest way out.

Those without minor children may consider getting a divorce without a lawyer. This is appropriate for those couples who have no money to speak of. Many states have DIY procedures that are easily followed. State courts give out forms for the couple to complete and printed material explaining the procedure to follow in order to get a divorce.

You can learn about the different state methods of obtaining a DIY divorce by researching on the Internet. There are web sites that list DIY divorce procedures by state. Just type in DIVORCE in your favorite search engine and you will pull up more web sites than you probably have time to explore.

Couples with a pre-nuptial agreement and no minor children can divorce without employing a lawyer, provided they have no problem living up to that agreement. If one of them decides to challenge that agreement, the other would be foolish to try to represent himself.

Divorce is a more complicated procedure for those who have minor children. The state considers that it has a duty to protect children when parents divorce. Actually, the state's interest in protecting a child is monetary. If the court does not require each parent to contribute to the child's support, the custodial parent may be forced to turn to the state for financial or medical assistance. It is the judge's job to see that doesn't happen.

That was brought home to me when I represented a young man who had two small children and a wife with a drug problem. He still cared for his wife, but he felt it best that they divorce and he assume full responsibility for the children. His wife did not contest the divorce. She didn't even show up when we went to court.

At court I explained that the wife had a drug problem and had virtually abandoned the children. "Judge, my client is asking for full custody of the children. The grandparents will help care for them while he is at work. My client is willing to assume full financial responsibility for their support."

The judge answered "Well, I am not willing to allow him to assume full financial responsibility. The child's mother is equally responsible to provide for the maintenance of her children. I am ordering that she contribute $200 a month for their support. I am granting the divorce and full custody to the father with no visitation rights for the mother."

When we left the courthouse, my client was annoyed. "$200 a month. That's a joke. She spend every penny she gets on drugs. He can order anything he likes, but getting her to obey that order is going to be his problem, not mine."

The reader may think the wife came out alright without a lawyer. But she didn't. The judge ordered her to pay $200 a month that she didn't have. Her children were virtually taken from her. She had no money to employ a lawyer, but she could have asked Legal Services for help. Had she been represented, her lawyer could have argued that she wasn't working and that she not be required to pay anything for several months until she was able to work. He could have argued that she be allowed supervised visits with her children.

True, the husband seemed disinclined to try to force his wife to pay $200 a month. But she came away from that divorce owing money to support children that she had no legal right to see. If at some later date she was able to turn her life around, her former husband could require her to make all of the back payments. He might decide to enforce the court's order and not allow any visits with the children. That could well be the case if he remarried and wanted to have his children establish a maternal relationship with their step-mother.

The point is, when minor children are involved, regardless of financial circumstances, it is important that each parent be represented by an attorney.

You Broke The Law 5

Unless you are a career criminal, you probably don't know a criminal attorney, none-the-less Mr. Right Criminal Attorney. If you are picked up for a crime, you may not have the opportunity to shop for an attorney. In such case, you may need to rely on your family to hire someone for you.

Those charged with a serious crime need a lawyer and fast! A good lawyer may be able to get the charge reduced. That was the case with Hank. He was stopped for drunk driving. He cussed out the police officer, and took a swing at him. Hank caused no harm. All he did was brush the officer's jacket. But the policeman took offense and charged him with felony battery on a police officer.

Lucky for Hank, he was able to employ Mr. Right Criminal Lawyer who explained to the prosecuting attorney that Hank had never been in trouble with the law. He was just having a bad time. He recently lost his job and his wife walked out on him. Hank was genuinely contrite and wanted to apologize to the officer. By then the police officer had cooled down and agreed that no harm had been done, so the charge was reduced to a misdemeanor of disorderly conduct.

Even if being booked for a lesser charge is not a possibility, still it is important that an attorney be employed as early as possible to preserve evidence. For example, it may be important to get a copy of the 911 tape. These tapes are erased after a period of time. It may take a Court order to preserve that tape. If you delay in employing an attorney, you may lose the opportunity to collect evidence favorable to your case. That's one of the problems with having a Court appointed attorney. It may be two or three weeks before you ever meet him.

DIY?

You have probably heard the saying "Whoever represents himself has a fool for a client." That certainly applies to the person who is charged with a serious crime. You should not even talk to the police, or any investigative authority without first consulting with your lawyer.

Two cases in point: The parents of Jon Benet immediately employed an attorney, who I have no doubt, advised them not to talk to the police. People thought the parents must know something about the crime, else why would they employ a lawyer so quickly? There were all sorts of rumors and speculation about the role of the parents in the crime that continues to this very day. But what people think won't put you in jail. The law gives you the right to remain silent; and that's exactly what they did and what you should do until you are able to consult with your attorney.

Second case: Martha Stewart. She was convicted, not of any crime, but of lying to investigators. Whatever was she thinking? She is an intelligent woman. Why did she even agree to talk to them? No doubt she thought she had done nothing wrong and therefore had nothing to hide. But she would not have been convicted if her attorney refused to allow her to be questioned in the first place.

THE MISDEMEANOR

It may be that you are picked up for a minor offense. In such case you may wonder whether you need an attorney. For first-time minor offenses, the answer might be "No." Most states offer a Pretrial Diversion Program for minor offenses. A common example is the traffic offense that results in an accident. Instead of racking up points, the first-time offender can go to traffic school. Your state may have a Pretrial Diversion Program for shoplifters, or for possession of a small amount of marijuana. If you were caught committing a minor crime and you are a first time offender, you might ask whether a Pretrial Diversion Program is available to you.

Those who qualify don't need an attorney to enter such program, still you may want to consult with a lawyer who can explain all of the legal consequences of pleading guilty and accepting a Pretrial Diversion Program. Increasingly, people who are convicted of a misdemeanor are suffering *collateral consequences* — which is lawyer talk for unpleasant things that happen in addition to the punishment given for the crime.

The most common example of a collateral consequence is the case of the person who is charged with going through a stop sign. If he is found guilty of this misdemeanor, his insurance company will take his conviction as proof that his is not driving safely. They will feel justified in increasing his car insurance premium because of his "bad" driving record. But the fine for going through the stop sign may be nothing compared to the increased cost of his car insurance.

Other collateral consequences of being convicted of a misdemeanor depends to a large degree on state law and the type of misdemeanor. If you are aged, conviction of a relatively minor driving offense may cause you to lose your driver's license. If you are convicted of shoplifting, your gun permit may be revoked. Conviction of possession of a small quantity of marijuana may cause you to lose your job. Those who live in California could be sent to jail for a minor offense under their "Three Strikes And You Are Out of Society" law. Any conviction can cause an immigrant to face deportation.

It is important to contact an experienced criminal attorney if you are charged with an offense, not only to learn of the punishment if convicted, but to learn of possible collateral consequences. You may decide to employ a lawyer to fight a misdemeanor just to avoid its collateral consequence.

FINDING MR. RIGHT

As recommended in the first chapter, it's important to call or interview at least three lawyers. You might call three criminal lawyers, two of whom make no promises but the third says "Don't worry, I can get you off." That may be what you want to hear, but he may be the wrong attorney for you. An experienced attorney knows that many facts can come to light when he starts his investigation. There is no way he can know the probable outcome of your case until he conducts a full investigation. Even then, he may not be able to predict the jury's verdict.

Past performance is no indication of whether a lawyer will be successful. The lawyer you're interviewing may brag "I got my last ten clients off without any penalty whatsoever." That may be true, but each case stands on its own. Your case may be the one to break his winning streak.

This holds for famous and successful lawyers as well. F. Lee Bailey is an example. He had an impressive string of wins before representing Pattie Hearst. Still, he lost that case and she went to jail.

Also be wary of the attorney who says: "I know the judge in this case. He and I are friends." In all probability the judge is also friends with the prosecuting attorney. Just the fact that your lawyer knows the judge, may not help you at all.

The reader may be wondering "Didn't I just read about an affair between a judge and a lawyer, and how the judge always ruled in the lawyer's favor?"

Yes, but the lawyer didn't brag about the relationship. Lawyers who have a "special friend" on the bench keep it quiet. It is illegal to have a judge rule in favor of a lawyer for any reason other than the law. You would do better to employ an attorney who says "I have been before that judge many times. Based on his past rulings, you will probably get probation."

THE RETAINER AGREEMENT

Criminal attorneys often offer a fixed price to represent a client who has been charged with a given crime. You need to get a feeling for the "going price" for defending against whatever charge has been filed against you. If this is your first brush with the law you may have no idea what is a realistic fee for defending you. You need to call or visit at least three experienced lawyers. If two say their fee is $10,000 and the third says $3,500, it may be wise to eliminate the $3,500 offer.

A lawyer must budget his time and effort if he is going to make a living. If you employ the lawyer with the lowest price, he may cut corners and that might result in a poor outcome for you. This is not a time to hunt for bargains.

Many criminal lawyers offer a Staged Fee Agreement as was described in the last Chapter. They have a flat fee for the initial investigation, another for work done up to the court plea, or dismissal, and then a fee for going to trial.

With a staged fee agreement, you need to be realistic about going to the next stage. If you were caught committing a crime on video tape, and admitted your guilt when you were arrested, why pay $20,000 to go to trial? You know you are guilty. Have your attorney use his best efforts to get a reduced charge or a lesser sentence.

The discussion in Chapter 2 relating to costs applies when you employ a criminal attorney. Your retainer agreement needs to identify what costs will be charged and how much will be charged for those costs.

An open-ended cost agreement is just as undesirable as an open-ended fee agreement. If your lawyer will not agree to a fixed price cost agreement, then have your retainer agreement state that he will not incur any extraordinary cost (such as an expert witness) without first obtaining your written approval. At least it won't be a shock to you when he sends a cost bill at the end of the month.

LOYALTY

Just because you know you are innocent, doesn't mean that the judge will believe you. In our system of justice, there is no guarantee that the good guy will go free or that the bad guy will be punished. All you are guaranteed is notice (you are told what the charge is) and a fair hearing.

Whether you are guilty or innocent of the charge is almost immaterial to the criminal lawyer. He is going to fight to get you off, no matter what. Still, whether he believes in your innocence can affect the way he represents you. You need to get some idea of how much he believes in your case. The usual tip-off is whether he expects you to be convicted. If you are innocent and your lawyer indicates that he expects you to be convicted, he may not be Mr. Right. You need someone who believes in you and who will take the time and effort to do whatever is necessary to gather sufficient evidence to clear you.

The investigative process is the most important part of your representation. Cases are won (or lost) before anyone steps into the court room. Evidence is the key to whether you will walk away a free person. You need to ask your lawyer how he intends to investigate your case. What plan does he have to collect evidence? Does he have a special investigator who he regularly employs, or does he do his own investigation? Will expert witnesses be needed in your case? If so, you need an estimate of what it will cost to have them testify on your behalf.

COMPATIBILITY

Bad enough you're fighting the system, you don't need to fight your lawyer as well. It won't help you. Picking a fight with your lawyer is like picking the "Go directly to jail" card in the game of Monopoly. The best way to defend against your lawyer is not to have a battle in the first place. Try to chose someone you feel you can work with, and then try to cooperate with him as much as you can.

One way to avoid disagreements is to get a clear understanding of what your attorney is going to do to help you. He needs to take the time to explain each step in the process. He needs to tell you what to expect and when to expect it.

CHOOSE A LAWYER YOU CAN CONFIDE IN

It's been said that there are two people that you should never lie to: your doctor and your lawyer. Lying to your doctor can lead to a misdiagnosis. Lying to your criminal attorney could land you in jail. And there is no reason to lie to your lawyer. We have this wonderful thing in our system of justice called attorney-client privilege. Whatever you tell your lawyer goes no further. Your lawyer is bound by law not to reveal anything you tell him in confidence.

Free communication between you and your lawyer is paramount if he is going to help you. He needs to know all of the facts, especially those facts that are damaging to your case. If he thinks the facts you reveal will result in conviction, he will probably ask you to allow him to negotiate a lighter sentence than you would get by going to trial.

Your lawyer can prepare for almost anything that you tell him. What he can't prepare for is what he doesn't know. You need to tell him everything that may impact your case. If not, he may be surprised at trial. And if there is one thing criminal lawyers hate, it's surprises.

That's what happened to Richard. The court assigned him to defend a case. He met with his client and learned the details leading up to the crime:

Phyllis had to go to the doctor. She was seven months pregnant with her third child and not feeling well. She wasn't up to traveling with her two year old and three year old, so she asked her mother to come over and baby sit. Her mother said "You know Bobbie don't want me round."

"Yeah, but I hafta go to the clinic. I just can't carry the kids with me. Bobbie got a job laying cinder block at that new mall construction. I'll be back way before him."

"O.K. It's been long since I seen the kids. I really miss them. . . . I'll bring some doughnuts."

It took Phyllis longer than she expected to get to the clinic. She wasn't able to move quickly so she missed the bus and had to wait a half hour for the next one. She was concerned when it started to drizzle. Bobbie might leave work early if it rained. She had to wait over an hour to see the doctor. He wanted some blood tests and an ultrasound. That took another hour, meanwhile the drizzle turned into a steady downpour. Phyllis was getting nervous, but she knew Bobbie would stop at the bar. It was rare for him to get home much before dark on a work day.

The rain was making Catherine nervous as well. She had enough run-ins with Bobbie to be wary of his temper. She heard the keys in the door and was relieved thinking it was Phyllis. But it was Bobbie.

"What are you doing here?"

Catherine tried to explain "Phyl had to go the doctor. She wasn't feeling well . . . "

Just then Phyllis came in. She could see that Bobbie had been drinking.

"I told you I don't want this bitch in my house."

"I needed to go the doctor. I can't carry two kids with this big belly."

The children picked up on the tension and began to cry. Their crying and Phyllis yelling at him, set Bobbie off. He smacked Phyllis hard across her face "Don't you talk back to me."

Catherine picked up a paring knife on the kitchen counter and jabbed Bobbie in his chest. He went straight down.

Phyllis screamed "Call 911."

The paramedics were there within minutes, but the blade had pierced Bobbie's heart and they could not revive him.

Catherine was in shock "It was an accident. I just wanted to stop him from hitting Phyllis. I didn't want to kill him." The police were sympathetic, but they still booked her for manslaughter.

Catherine had no money, so the court appointed Richard as her attorney. She cried when she told Richard about the years of abuse her daughter had suffered. Richard consoled her. "You were defending your daughter and unborn grandchild. No jury would convict you of manslaughter."

What Catherine didn't tell her lawyer was about the strained relationship between her and her daughter. Catherine was against the marriage from the beginning. She didn't even attend the wedding. After the marriage, all she did was bad-mouth Bobbie. And that was easy to do. He had no steady job. He spent his days drinking and yelling at Phyllis and the kids. Phyllis made excuses for Bobbie. Catherine criticized Phyllis for staying in the marriage.

Bobbie blamed his mother-in-law for causing trouble in their marriage. Eventually, Phyllis came to agree with him.

Richard was not surprised when the prosecution said they were going to call Phyllis as a witness. After all, she did see her mother stab Bobbie. He spoke to Phyllis before the trial, but, like her mother, she gave no indication that she and her mother were estranged.

What a surprise when she testified!
- Yes, Bobbie hit her, but it was only a slap.

- No, he never hurt her or any of their children.

- Yes, he did drink on occasion, but he was no alcoholic.

- Yes, her mother argued with Bobbie on many occasions.

- No, she and Bobbie did not have marital problems, just mother-in-law problems.

By the end of her testimony Phyllis was sobbing that now her three babies were going to have to grow up without a daddy.

Catherine got twenty years to life.

UNCLE HENRY LEFT YOU MONEY

6

Most people who inherit money consider it to be "pennies from heaven" and are grateful for anything they get. Usually the only thing they want to know is "How much am I going to get?" and "When am I going to get it?" What most people do not appreciate until well into the Probate proceedings, is that the answer to these two questions depends in large measure on the laws of the state, the person appointed to settle the affairs of the *decedent* (the person who died) and of course, his lawyer.

The *Probate Estate* is that part of the decedent's property that needs to be transferred to a beneficiary by means of a court procedure. In most states, the person appointed by the court to settle the Estate is called the *Personal Representative.* The court will appoint the person named in the Will to serve as Personal Representative. If there is no Will, the judge will appoint whoever has priority according to state law. Generally, that's the surviving spouse, or if no spouse, his children.

Whoever is appointed as Personal Representative needs to employ a lawyer to guide him through the Probate procedure. It is the lawyer's job to see that all the rules relating to the Probate procedure are followed, and at no personal liability to the Personal Representative. In other words, the lawyer's job is to protect the Personal Representative from spending any of his own money to settle the Estate.

All expenses (including attorney fees) are paid from Uncle Henry's Estate. The beneficiaries get whatever is left once all the bills and expenses are paid. The Personal Representative hires the lawyer, but it's the beneficiaries who are really paying the lawyer's fee.

Talk about your conflict of interest. The beneficiaries pay for a lawyer they didn't employ and over whom they have no control!

In most cases, the Personal Representative is a major beneficiary of the Estate, so there is no actual conflict of interest. He uses Estate funds to pay the lawyer, but it is coming out of his own pocket. If the Personal Representative is not a major beneficiary of Uncle Henry's Estate, you very well might have a problem with conflict of interest. That being the case, we are entitling this section

How To Defend Against The Personal Representative's Lawyer

Legislators have long been aware of the potential for abuse, not only in attorney's fees, but in Personal Representative fees. Like his lawyer, the Personal Representative is entitled to be paid for his efforts in settling the Estate. In many states, a fee schedule is set by law. It is usually a percentage of the value of the Probate Estate. In other states, all the law requires is that these fees be "reasonable." TRANSLATION: whatever is the going rate in the community and/or whatever the judge thinks is reasonable.

In all states, attorney and Personal Representative fees are subject to court approval. If you are a beneficiary of the Estate and you think too much is being paid to the Personal Representative, or his lawyer, you can go to court and ask the judge to reduce that fee. But you better take your own lawyer with you.

If there is one thing a judge dislikes is someone who comes before his court without a lawyer. Judges are sworn to uphold the law and to protect the rights of the citizens. You are putting the judge in the uncomfortable position of trying to be impartial and at the same time protecting your rights. It's a conflict of interests.

Being a judge he will probably go with trying to be impartial. He will listen to the legal arguments of the attorney for the Personal Representative. Unless you have some legal background, you will not have your own legal argument to present as a counter-balance.

Expect to lose.

Do you know what is worse than losing? Having the Personal Representative and his lawyer charge the Estate (that's your money) for the time they had to go to court to argue against you!

Are you beginning to feel helpless? You might need to get used to that feeling depending on where the Probate is being conducted.

The rights of a beneficiary vary significantly state to state. In some states, you don't have the right to be notified of how the Probate is being conducted unless you make a written request to the court (on the proper form) for a copy of everything filed during Probate. Some states have laws that give specific rights to the beneficiaries, but even in those states, the Personal Representative is still in charge of the Probate proceeding.

Some readers may be thinking that the best way to protect his interest as a beneficiary is to get himself appointed as Personal Representative, but that may not be possible unless you have priority under the laws of the state. As explained, top priority goes to the person named in the Will to serve as the *Executor* or Personal Representative of the Will. If the decedent did not leave a valid Will, his next of kin have the right to be appointed as Personal Representative.

The next of kin are defined by the state's *Laws of Intestate Succession*. In some states, they are called the *Laws of Descent and Distribution*. The surviving spouse is the next of kin with top priority. If there is no spouse, or the spouse cannot or will not serve, the decedent's children are next in line for the job. If there is more than one child, they can decide among themselves who will serve as Personal Representative. If they can't agree, the court will make the decision, but that will involve a court battle. If there is one message, the reader should come away with after reading this book, is that a court battle is a good thing to avoid.

Because most Personal Representatives have no idea of what needs to be done to settle an Estate, it is really his lawyer who is in charge. No wonder books are written about how to avoid Probate.

If you are going to be Personal Representative, you need to look for Mr. Right Probate Lawyer, but before doing so, you need to determine whether a Probate proceeding is necessary in the first place. There is no reason to go through a court procedure, if you can get possession of all the decedent owned.

You should be able to get possession of those items that were in his name only if he made some provision for an automatic transfer to a beneficiary. For example, he may have owned a bank account in his name "In Trust For" a named beneficiary. He could have held securities in his name only with instructions to "Transfer On Death" to a named beneficiary. The beneficiary should be able to get possession of these gifts by giving the company a certified copy of the death certificate.

Once you determine that there are items that need to be transferred by means of Probate, you can begin your search for Mr. Right Probate Lawyer. That you will be looking for someone experienced in Probate law, is a given. But having someone who is a specialist in Probate is not as important as finding someone who is honest.

You can get clues about whether the Probate lawyer is honest at your first meeting. He should ask many questions before he puts a retainer agreement in front of you. He should ask whether you expect any discord in the family about who is entitled to be appointed as Personal Representative or inherit the property.

He should ask what property needs to be transferred and where that property is located. If the decedent owns out of state property, you may need to conduct two Probate procedures. One in the state of his residence and one in the state where he owns property. The attorney should take the time to explain the pros and cons of beginning the Probate proceeding in the state of the decedent's residence.

The lawyer should be willing to take the time to explain the Probate procedure to you. And there isn't just one Probate procedure. Every state has different procedures for different size and types of estates. Most states allow *personal property* (bank accounts, securities, etc.) to be transferred without going through a Probate, provided the amount is no greater than that allowed by law and the beneficiary signs an *Affidavit* (a written statement sworn to before a notary public) verifying that he is entitled to the property. In California that amount is $100,000 but in other states, it is a lot less. Just about every state requires some sort of Probate procedure to transfer *real property* (land, condominiums, houses, etc.) owned by the decedent in his name only.

Many states allow shortened Probate procedures called *Summary Administration* for small Estates with no creditor problems. These shortened procedures are less expensive than a full Probate procedure. The attorney should explain which of these different types of Probate procedures are available to you. He should also give you some idea of how long it will take to complete that procedure.

You can often determine honesty by the amount of information that the lawyer reveals to you about non-Probate transfers and shortened Probate procedures. Give him a plus, if he offers this information without the need for you to ask for it. Give him a minus if you need to ask these questions and he gives you a vague or incomplete answer.

Don't decide that the lawyer you are interviewing is Mr. Right until you carefully read his retainer agreement. All the things we said about open-ended retainer agreements apply. If he is experienced, the lawyer should know how much time he is going to spend on the whole procedure. Try to negotiate a fixed priced agreement. If he tells you he is going to charge the *statutory fee* (that allowed under state law) ask him for a copy of that law. There is no law that says he must get what the law allows. Statutes relating to fees are only guidelines. The judge can award the attorney more if the Probate is complicated because of a disagreement about what bills need to be paid, or who is to inherit the property. It rarely happens, but the judge can reduce the fee if the lawyer does a poor job.

Statutory fees are not set in stone. You can negotiate a price lower than that allowed by law. If there are no statutory guidelines, try to negotiate an upper limit fee agreement. — one that says that no additional fee will be charged unless the attorney needs to spend more than a certain amount of time to complete the Probate.

Don't bother to try to negotiate a lower hourly rate. If he wants $200 an hour and you get him to agree to $100 an hour, expect that he will take twice as long to do the work. There is no way you can determine whether it took him an hour to prepare a document or whether he did it in a half hour.

Don't be tempted to skip all of these safety checks just because the attorney represented you in the past. That was the mistake Ethel made.

Her husband was looking at the pictures taken of his 84th birthday party. He was surprised to see how old he looked. Round shouldered, stooped over, wrinkled smile. Strange how a picture shows things you never see in the mirror. He said "Babe, we're getting old."

Ethel laughed "You haven't called me Babe since we were kids."

But Jeff was somber . "We probably don't have much more time together. We need to set things in order."

Ethel made light of his concern. "You may be getting old, but not me." She turned her head as she said it. She didn't want him to see the tears in her eyes.

Jeff asked his card-playing buddies at the condo if they knew a good lawyer to write a Will. "There's a law firm right on Main Street. They look expensive, but they're not. A lot of the work is done by their legal assistant, so I guess that's how they keep the price down."

Jeff and Ethel had their lawyer prepare a "sweetheart" Will for each of them. The one that goes "I give everything that I own to my spouse. If my spouse shall not survive me, then I give all that I own to our child . . ."

Less than two months later Jeff died suddenly from a massive heart attack. Ethel was in shock. They'd been together since they were children. He was everything to her. How could she manage without him? She turned to the lawyer who just drafted their Wills "Don't you worry. I will take care of everything. We will file Jeff's Will with the Probate court to begin the Probate procedure."

She signed a retainer agreement for $225 per hour. He told her that any work done by his legal assistance would be at $175 per hour. That seemed reasonable to Ethel, so she gave him a check for $1,000 to cover the cost of the Probate filing fees and his time to begin the Probate procedure.

Each month Ethel would get a bill from the lawyer that outlined in detail, all of the things that were being done to Probate Jeff's Will. Six months and five thousand dollars later, the lawyer called and said he was getting ready to close the Estate. Ethel asked "When do I get the money?"

"You already have all the money. Everything Jeff owned was held jointly with you."

"Then why did we need to go through Probate?"

"There was a lot that had to be done to settle Jeff's Estate. I had to publish a Notice To Creditors to make sure that Jeff didn't owe any money. You know in this state, if Jeff died owing money, his creditors would have the right to sue you for the money."

"How could Jeff owe anything? We always paid cash."

"I had to file his final income tax return."

"Our accountant always took care of tax returns, and at a lot less than $225 an hour."

"I had to notify Social Security, and Jeff's pension fund."

"I could have done that."

The lawyer said he was sorry that Ethel felt that way, but he had done his job according to their retainer agreement.

Ethel was angry. She felt she was taken advantage of at a time when she was most vulnerable. She called the state Bar to complain about the lawyer. The lawyer at the Bar was sympathetic, but he reminded her that she did sign a retainer agreement and her lawyer did live up to that agreement.

Ethel said "You mean there's nothing I can do?"

"No, I didn't say that. You can consult with a different attorney who may be able to help you. I can refer you to an attorney in your area who is very well respected in the legal community."

Ethel met with that attorney who turned out to be Mr. Right. He was outraged at what had been done. "All lawyers are required to take ethics courses. This lawyer must have slept through the whole class."

"Can I get my money back?"

"There are several ways we could go, but since the Probate is still ongoing, the best way is to ask the judge of the Probate court to disallow all attorney fees. I will need to file a petition objecting to his attorney fees. I will ask the court to set a hearing on the matter. You can be present at the hearing if you like." Mr. Right explained that it would take several hours to prepare the petition, file it with the court, set it for hearing, attend the hearing, explain the problem to the judge, and then hopefully, to see that the money was returned. He offered to do all this work for a fee of $1,000.

Ethel agreed and did attend the hearing. She expected that the lawyer would be ashamed of what he had done and that he would readily agree to returning the money. Boy was she mistaken!

Mr. Wrong vigorously argued that Ethel employed him to settle Jeff's Estate and that was exactly what he did. They had a valid retainer agreement. He had performed according to that agreement. He was entitled to be paid for his efforts. Mr. Right argued that the retainer agreement was for the Probate of Jeff's Estate. Since Ethel did not profit in any way from the Probate procedure she should not have to pay attorney's fees for that Probate.

Mr. Wrong argued back. "I performed a lot of services for my client. She was so distraught at the death of her husband that she was unable to take care of all the things that needed to be done. She needed my assistance."

After a half hour of arguments back and forth , the judge finally ruled. "Had your retainer agreement explained that you were going to assist your client in settling her husband's affairs, then it would have been proper for her to pay you for these efforts. But your retainer agreement was for the Probate of her husband's Estate. There was no reason to open a Probate Estate because the decedent owned nothing in his name only. Because the value of the Probate Estate is zero, that's what I am awarding you. You are hereby ordered to refund all of the monies paid to you."

WILLS, TRUSTS
AND WHO NOT TO TRUST

7

Several months after her father's death Ethel's daughter, Laurie, came in for a visit. She was concerned about her mother's health. The doctor said she had high blood pressure, diabetes and heart problems. She was also worried about the way her mother was dealing with the loss of her father. Her mother seemed irritable and depressed. Some days she wouldn't answer the phone. Other days, she would be lonely and call Laurie several times.

Ethel was happy to see her daughter. This visit was just what she needed. Laurie was surprised to see how well she looked. They enjoyed each other's company, going shopping and afterward to a movie. Ethel insisted on paying for the tickets. She laughed "You know you're getting old when you pay senior citizen price for your daughter."

The topic of aging came up more than once during Laurie's visit. Ethel was proud of the fact that she was 82, still driving, still living independently. Laurie didn't ask, but she wondered how her mother was managing her finances now that her father was gone.

Ethel was never open about her finances. Laurie didn't know what her mother owned. Her mother seemed to live well enough, but Ethel was a squirrel with money — always saving for the winter.

Maybe her mother had a lot of money, maybe none. Laurie had no way of knowing; but being an only child, she felt she at least had the right to ask about what provisions were made in the event her mother died.

"I know Dad and you owned everything jointly, so when he died everything was taken care of. Have you set things up in the same way?"

"I have a Will. You are my only beneficiary. Don't worry you will be taken care of."

"But you remember the problem you had with Dad's Probate. I heard that there are many ways to avoid Probate, like setting up a Trust."

"That lying thief of a lawyer. He should have told me I didn't need to go through Probate in the first place."

"Maybe we should talk to that nice lawyer, who helped get your money back, just to see if all of your finances are in order."

"No. I've had it with lawyers. I had to pay him $1,000 just to get my own money back. I told you I have a Will. Everything is taken care of. Don't rush me. You'll get your money soon enough."

That really hurt Laurie.

She wasn't trying to get her mother's money. She was just trying to be sure that she didn't go through the same nightmare her mother suffered when her father died.

Laurie never raised the topic again. It was unfortunate that her mother closed her mind to consulting with an Estate Planning attorney. He could have suggested any number of methods that Ethel could have used to avoid having her daughter go through Probate.

When Ethel died the following year, Laurie was left with a mess. She didn't know what her mother owned. She tried to get the bank to let her enter her mother's safe deposit box, but the bank officer refused. "The safe deposit box is in your mother's name only. We can't let you remove the contents of the box without a court order."

"How do I get an order?"

"I don't know. Most people get a lawyer to help."

Laurie turned to the Probate lawyer who had helped her mother to get her $5,000 back. He got a court order allowing them to examine the contents of her mother's safe deposit box. They found securities in the box worth well over $300,000. All of them were in Ethel's name only. Laurie would need to go through Probate in order to have the securities transferred to her name.

Laurie's lawyer was honest and competent; but it still took a full Probate proceeding costing over $20,000, and more than a year to settle her mother's Estate.

Some readers may not be sympathetic. What's the problem? Laurie cleared $280,000, didn't she?

The point is that the $300,000 was Laurie's inheritance. It should not have been necessary for her to pay a lawyer to get what was already hers. Simple action on Ethel's part could have avoided Probate.

The irony is that Ethel hated Probate lawyers. Yet the only one to profit by Ethel's refusal to set up an Estate Plan was a Probate lawyer. In fact, the best way to help your beneficiaries defend against a Probate lawyer is to set up an Estate Plan that avoids the need for Probate altogether. You may need to employ an Estate Planning attorney to help you do so. This being the case, we are naming this section: **How To Defend Against Your Estate Planning Lawyer**

Some readers may be ready to skip over to the next chapter thinking that only rich people go to Estate Planning attorneys. And there are lawyers who specialize in Estate Planning for the wealthy, but we are using the term to refer to any attorney who helps people plan for the orderly transfer of their property to named beneficiaries.

In other words, any lawyer who prepares a Will or Trust is engaging in the area of law referred to as Estate Planning.

Lawyers who have a general practice often write Wills and Trusts as part of that practice. When looking for Mr. Right Estate Planning Lawyer you need to determine whether he is experienced in the field.

EXPERIENCE

Every state has laws relating to what is, and what is not, proper to include in a Will. Every state has laws saying how a Will should be signed and witnessed. A lengthy, and expensive court battle can result if state law is not followed. An ambiguous Will that can be interpreted in two ways, or one that is signed when the Will maker isn't quite with it, can be challenged once the Will maker dies.

A lawyer who writes a Will or a Trust needs to be both skilled and experienced. Estate Planning lawyers have the proper training and experience to write such documents. If you go to a general practitioner to write your Will or Trust, you need to ask whether he has taken courses relating to Estate Planning. Asking what percentage of his practice is devoted to writing Wills and Trusts might not help you. He could be preparing the same poorly drafted document over and over again.

You may get some indication of his Estate Planning skills from the way he conducts your initial interview. A good attorney will want to get to know you. He will want to know the extent of your wealth so that he can advise whether a Trust is appropriate to transfer your wealth, or whether a simple Will is sufficient. He will want to know what you are trying to accomplish. Are you just interested in giving away your money when you're gone, or is there someone you want to care for even when you are no longer here? Give him a minus if he leaves the important task of information gathering to his legal assistant.

No matter what your goal, your lawyer should include a discussion about how you can avoid Probate in this first meeting. Give your lawyer several minus points if he doesn't mention Probate.

HONESTY

I knew a lawyer who had a vault full of original Wills that he was storing for his clients. He referred to the Wills as "money in the bank." To him, the vault was a treasure of future earnings. He expected that when the Will maker died, his family members would come to him to get the original Will, and when they did, he would be employed to do the Probate.

So he drafted as many Wills as he could, for a very reasonable price — less than any other lawyer in town. But when it came to the Probate, he was the most expensive lawyer in town.

This lawyer always advised his client to make a Will — whether they needed it or not. For example, a new client moved in from another state and showed him a Will that was prepared in the other state. The out-of-state Will was signed in the presence of two witnesses and a notary public, yet this lawyer strongly recommended that a new one be written that "will be good in this state."

What the lawyer didn't explain was that each state respects the laws of other states. A Will that is properly drafted and signed according to the laws of the state of the Will maker's residence should be valid in all other states. Even if, for some reason, that Will is not accepted in the new state, the beneficiaries can always take the Will back to the state where it was drafted and have it Probated there.

What the client should have done is ask exactly why it was necessary to draft a new Will. But he was from the "father knows best" generation, so he had the lawyer prepare a new Will. Besides, this lawyer didn't charge much and he was a most congenial fellow, taking the time to chat with his clients about everything — except how to avoid Probate.

Once the Will was signed, the lawyer suggested that he store his client's original Will "for safe keeping." The client thought it very nice of his lawyer to be so concerned about the safety of his Will.

The Will lawyer never asked his client about how much money he had. He charged his Probate fees as a percentage of the value of the deceased client's property. If his client was rich, so much the better. He'd earn more money when the client died.

There was another lawyer in town who specialized in Estate Planning. Unlike the Will lawyer, he charged a premium for his services, which consisted mostly of writing Trusts. Like the Will lawyer, he was not interested in knowing much about the client's goals or the extent of his wealth.

Regardless of whether his client was rich or of modest means, he'd give him the same sales pitch "It's really important to avoid Probate. The best way to do so is to set up a Revocable Living Trust. The way you set up a Trust is to sign a Trust Agreement naming yourself as the Trustee of the Trust. You can put your property into your Trust by changing ownership from yourself individually to you, as the Trustee of your Revocable Living Trust. For example, if you have a bank account in your name, you can put it in your name 'as Trustee.' During your lifetime you have complete control of that bank account just as if it were in your name only."

He explained how the Trust could be used to transfer property to a beneficiary without the need for Probate.

"Should you become incapacitated, or die, whoever you name as your Successor Trustee will take over. Your Trust Agreement will tell your Successor Trustee how to manage the Trust. You can tell him that once you die, he is to give all of the Trust property to those you name as beneficiaries of the Trust and he will do so without the need to go through Probate."

Once the client signed the Trust Agreement, it was up to him to transfer his property into his Trust. The lawyer offered no assistance. If for some reason, the client kept property in his name only, a Probate procedure would be necessary to transfer the property to the proper beneficiary. The Trust lawyer figured the only thing better than getting big bucks to draft the Trust was to get paid for the Probate as well.

There was still another Estate Planning lawyer who prided himself in being a Certified Financial Planner who was licensed to sell insurance and securities. Like the Trust Lawyer, he was interested in selling Trusts. He was also interested in selling stocks, bonds and insurance. He didn't care what the client bought, just so long as he got his legal fees and/or a commission from the sale.

All of the lawyers we have described were dishonest, but they were boy scouts compared to the next Mr. Wrong.

Randolph was a self-made man. He started as a stockbroker, graduated into mortgage banking, and eventually founded his own firm. He was a good worker and a better employer. The average length of employment in his company was well over 20 years. Hugh, the company attorney, had been with him for longer than that. Randolph considered Hugh to be more of a friend and confident than his lawyer.

He would tell Hugh when he and his wife, Ellen were on the outs. Mostly it was over their son, Randolph, Jr. Randy was close to his mother, but he was a disappointment to his father.

The father constantly criticized the boy. His school grades were good, but did not live up to his father's expectation. The boy was not interested in sports, so there were no father and son outings to football or baseball games. They had nothing in common.

When Ellen allowed Randy to enroll in dance school, Randolph accused her of causing their son to be effeminate. Truth was, Randolph could not accept the fact that his son was gay.

Randy eventually graduated from college and became successful as an accountant. His father did not invite him to join his firm. He felt that anyone who lived "that" life style couldn't be trusted to manage money.

One day Randolph was diagnosed with lung cancer. He seemed to age overnight. Hugh suggested that he help Randolph "put things in order" by setting up a Trust for his wife and son.

Randolph was much too ill to understand the Trust that Hugh put in front of him to sign. It was over 30 pages long and was written in pure legalese, but he trusted his long time employee and friend to do what was best for him and his family.

Hugh gave Randolph an abridged explanation of the Trust "While you are able, you are Trustee and in charge of the Trust. As soon as you sign it I will help you place everything you own into the Trust, including the business."

"Yes but I want to continue to run the business."

"As Trustee you are in complete control of everything in the Trust. You can do anything with your Trust property that you can now do. Buy, sell, spend, invest, anything. The only time your Successor Trustee takes over is when you are too sick to manage things. I know Ellen has never managed money; and you have no faith in Randy, so should you become too ill to manage Trust property, I will take over as Successor Trustee. In the event that I become incapacitated or die, I have provided for the Trust department at our local bank to serve as Successor Trustee."

"But will Ellen and Randy be able to access the money?"

"Of course, I made good provision for both of them. They will have more than enough money to live on. You know you are a very wealthy man. In fact, they probably will not be able to spend all of the money you earned during their lifetime. You need to name some charity to inherit your fortune once Ellen and Randy are gone."

Randolph had always been in complete control of the family finances. He never discussed money with either of them, so Ellen and Randy had no idea that Randolph had set up the Trust.

When Randolph died, Hugh explained that he was Successor Trustee. He assured them he would give them more than enough for their every day needs. There would be no change in their life style.

Randy demanded to see a copy of the Trust. He couldn't believe what he was reading. Hugh was in complete control of their finances. All he and his mother would receive was an income for life. They had no right to spend any of the principal of the Trust. Ellen was confused "What does all this mean?"

Randy explained "It's like me giving you a check for a million dollars, only you can't cash the check and spend it. All you can do is spend the interest that the million dollars earns each year. "

Ellen wondered "Is that so bad? Hugh has been a good friend. I'm sure he'll do what's right."

"No, you don't understand. What he did was wrong. He made himself Trustee. He uses Trust funds to pay himself to manage the Trust. He uses Trust funds to pay himself for any legal work he does. We don't have anything to say about how he spends Trust money. He is in complete control, not only of the Trust, but of Dad's business. He could run that business into the ground and we could only stand by helplessly."

Randy employed a lawyer to challenge the Trust. Hugh, being Trustee, used Trust funds to defend the Trust. That left Randy in the ridiculous position of using his Trust funds to prosecute AND defend the Trust. Worse yet, he had to go to court to force Hugh to give him enough money from the Trust to pay for his lawyer's fees.

Eventually, Randy did oust Hugh as Trustee. The court ruled that Hugh had used undue influence to get Randolph to appoint him as Trustee. The court left the Trust intact, but did allow Randy and Ellen to choose their own Trustee. By having the power to hire (and fire) the Trustee, Randy and Ellen regained a measure of control over their inheritance. But it was a costly battle, financially and emotionally.

It would be nice to say that things like this rarely happen, but that is not the case.

It is a conflict of interest for a lawyer to make himself a beneficiary or a Personal Representative of a Will that he writes. Similarly, it is a conflict of interest for a lawyer to write a Trust and name himself as a beneficiary, Trustee or Successor Trustee of that Trust. In some states, legislators have recognized the potential for abuse and have passed laws banning such action. But many states have no such ban, so it is up to the client to protect himself.

Defending Against
A Conflict Of Interest

There are four basic "Don'ts" to use to defend yourself and your beneficiaries from a conflict of interest with your Estate Planning attorney:

Rule 1.   Don't sign a Will or Trust unless you fully understand what each paragraph means.

Rule 2.   Don't allow your attorney to include a paragraph in your Will saying that you want him to be the lawyer for your Personal Representative. In some states, such a paragraph is illegal. The reason is obvious. Your Personal Representative should have the right to hire or fire his own lawyer. The same applies to a Trust. Your Successor Trustee should have the right to employ the lawyer of his choice to assist him in administering the Trust. Your Trust should not require him to employ the drafting lawyer.

Rule 3. Don't allow the lawyer who drafts your Will to name himself as you Personal Representative. The same principal applies to a Trust. Do not allow the lawyer who drafts the Trust to name himself as Trustee or Successor Trustee.

Rule 4. Don't have your drafting attorney include a gift to himself in your Will or Trust — even if that lawyer is related to you.

I can give you an example from personal experience. I am one of five children. My father asked me to draft his Will. I refused. I knew I would be a beneficiary of his Will. I knew he would probably want me to serve as Personal Representative. It would have been a conflict of interest for me to write the Will and to benefit from it as well.

And there was no reason for me to do so. Another attorney did a fine job in writing the Will. Because I did not draft the Will and was not present when it was signed, there was never any question that the choice of beneficiaries and the choice of Personal Representative was strictly that of my father.

My father gave all his children an equal share, so I was a beneficiary of his Will and I did get appointed as his Personal Representative. In conducting the Probate proceedings I wore two hats. I was Personal Representative of my father's estate and I was the attorney for the Personal Representative.

Yes, it was a conflict of interest. I could have paid myself as Personal Representative and I could have paid myself as lawyer for the Personal Representative.

Some states, such as Kentucky, do not allow such double-dipping. In Kentucky, you either get paid as the Personal Representative or as the attorney for the Personal Representative, but not both.

That's not the rule in Florida. Florida statute gives a schedule of fees that can be charged by the Personal Representative and a schedule of fees that can be charged by the attorney for the Personal Representative. These fees are most generous as compared to the fee schedules of other states.

Under Florida law, I could have paid myself under both fee schedules, but I didn't because I believe that Florida law is wrong and Kentucky law is right.

DIY PROBATE? 8

Whether you will be able to get Uncle Henry's property without employing a lawyer depends on Uncle Henry, and he's dead. When he was alive he had full control over the transfer of his property both before and after his death. If he had the foresight to arrange his finances so that all of his property can be transferred without Probate, then in most cases, all the beneficiary needs to do is produce a death certificate. That is the case with bank accounts that he held *in trust for* someone, or securities with a *transfer on death* designation.

If he neglected to make such arrangement, state law will dictate what procedure must be followed before any transfer can be made.

In most states, a small amount of personal property that is in the decedent's name only can be transferred to the proper beneficiary by means of an Affidavit prepared according to state law. The only problem is that states have different ideas about what is "small." As explained in Chapter 6, in California small is $100,000 or less, but in most other states, it is well under $50,000.

Most states have a shortened Probate procedure that can be done without a lawyer. Again there is great variation, state to state, about how the procedure is conducted, and the conditions under which the court will allow the shortened procedure.

Most Probate courts offer written material about shortened Probate procedures. It may be worthwhile to take a trip to the court house in the county of the decedent's residence to learn about what transfers are allowed without going through a full Probate procedure.

As always, there is the Internet. Because Probate procedures are so very different state to state, it is important to go to the state web site to learn of how things are done in that state.

Generally, a shortened Probate procedure is not the way to go if the decedent owed a lot of money. You will need to employ a lawyer who may need to ask the court to decide which debts need to be paid and how much each creditor is to receive. If beneficiaries transfer funds to themselves without making provision to pay the debt, creditors can later sue the beneficiary for that money.

In some states, creditors can even challenge transfers made from a joint bank account. The point is that DIY is not advisable if the decedent owed a significant amount of money. You need to consult with a Probate attorney to avoid the creditor holding you responsible for his debts. This is especially the case for a surviving spouse. In many states a creditor can demand payment from the spouse. A Probate attorney can explain whether the spouse is responsible to pay that debt or whether the creditor can collect from the decedent's Probate Estate only.

One unusual creditor problem happened in my own family. My aunt died at the age of 93. Her son had her admitted to a nursing home the year before she died. Although she was frail, she was able to sign all of the admission documents herself. By signing those documents she agreed to be liable to pay for her own nursing care, but she ran out of money before she died. The nursing home turned to her son for payment. He explained that although he had accompanied his mother to the home, he did not agree to pay for her nursing care, and he had no intention of doing so.

Strangely enough, my cousin died suddenly of a heart attack within a few months of his mother's death. All of his property was owned jointly with his wife, so no Probate procedure was necessary. But I received a concerned call from his wife saying that the nursing home was trying to charge his Estate for her mother-in-law's care!

This problem was easily solved because of two important factors. He never agreed to pay for his mother's care, and there was no Probate proceeding. Had there been a Probate, the creditor could have filed a claim against his Estate. It would have taken time, effort and attorney's fees to convince the court to disallow the claim.

Which is just another reason why it is important to avoid the need for Probate.

THE HOMEMADE WILL

The married couple who owns all of their property jointly have a DIY Estate Plan. Their plan is to have the surviving spouse take possession of all that they own, without the need to go through Probate. They still need to make plans for the orderly transfer of their property in the event they die simultaneously, say in a car crash. The simplest way to provide for such happening is to have a Will appointing someone to settle their affairs and naming beneficiaries to receive all that they own.

The reader may be thinking that a Will is a simple thing and why not write one out yourself? But writing a Will is like figure skating. It looks easy, but isn't. Each state has its own laws about what the state considers to be a valid Will. Some states allow a handwritten, unwitnessed Will to be filed for Probate, but most states will not allow property to be transferred based on such document.

A few states have a Will form included as part of their statutes. The residents of such states can copy the statutory Will, fill in the blanks and then have it witnessed according to the directions given.

But even in those states with statutory Wills, you need to think twice about DIY. Your DIY Will can be challenged on the basis that you didn't know what you were doing when you signed it.

If you have one of your beneficiaries witness your Will, someone may accuse him of using *undue influence* in getting you to sign the Will. In other words, he talked you into distributing your property according to his wishes, and not yours.

These problems can be avoided by having a lawyer prepare your Will. Should someone try to challenge your Will, your lawyer will be able to testify that he prepared the Will according to your wishes and that you knew exactly what you were doing when you signed it in his office. For a relatively small attorney fee, you should be able to avoid an expensive court battle over the validity of your Will.

Those with significant assets should consider employing Mr. Right Estate Planning Lawyer. He can suggest any number of ways to arrange your property so as to avoid Probate. One method commonly used is the Revocable Living Trust.

Those do-it-yourselfers may point out that there are any number of Trust kits on the market, so why bother with a lawyer? But if you read a Trust Agreement you will realize that it is a complex legal document. There are few people without a legal background who can fully understand the significance of each sentence of the document.

Some might say that there are companies that help the customer fill out the Trust Agreement. I refer to those companies as the "paper-filler-outers."

THE PAPER-FILLER-OUTERS

The equivalent in law to over-the-counter drugs is the rapidly growing population of "paper-filler-outers." These people and companies help customers complete legal forms. They are supposed to limit their services to just the completion of documents and not give legal advice. But the customer may ask legal questions related to that document. If the paper-filler-outer answers, that is giving legal advice.

Giving legal advice for a fee is what a licensed lawyer does. If he is not a lawyer, the paper-filler-outer could be prosecuted for the illegal, unlicensed, practice of law, so those who are reputable will not answer such a question.

But if he can't answer questions about the form he is helping you to complete, why pay for his services?

Maybe it is best that he doesn't answer. The person helping the customer to complete the document is not a lawyer. It's like asking the doctor's receptionist. "Should I take this drug?" You can get an answer, but it might not be the right one for you.

If you need someone to help you complete the document, chances are that you do not fully understand the legal effect of signing that document. In such case, you would do better to employ a lawyer to help you.

Also, you need to keep in mind that Estate Planning is more than drafting documents for you to sign. It is about developing an overall plan that helps you preserve your assets during your lifetime and then transfer them quickly and at minimum cost to the beneficiaries of your choice.

Mr. Right Estate Planning Lawyer can suggest any number of ways to help you achieve these worthy goals.

MEDICAL ASSISTANCE   9

A monthly luncheon was being held by the local church group. As was their custom, they invited a speaker to discuss something that would be of interest to the group. This day the topic was Elder Law and I was the speaker. I sat in the back of the room until they finished their preliminary business. One lady seated in front of me turned to her friend and asked "What's an Elder Law attorney?" She shrugged her shoulders and said "I think it's a bunch of old lawyers who get together to practice law."

True, my youth was far behind me, but the term Elder Law refers to what the attorney does and not to his age. An Elder Law attorney limits his practice to issues of the elderly, such as Estate Planning (Wills, Trusts, Powers of Attorney, etc.), guardianship or conservatorship, as the case may be in the given state. But their main focus is helping people qualify for Medicaid.

To the uninitiated, this may seem very strange. Isn't the Medicaid a Medical Assistance program funded by the state and federal government to provide health care for the poor? You mean that Elder Law attorneys help people to become poor so that they can qualify for Medicaid?

Well not exactly. It's a lot more complicated than that. To understand what Elder Law attorneys do and how this all evolved, we need to go back to the 1980's, and this author's personal experience.

I was attending law school at the time when my step-mother was diagnosed with Alzheimer's disease. Dad was not in the best health himself, having suffered a heart attack a few years earlier. But he cared for her at home for as long as he could. Eventually she needed round the clock care and Dad had to place her in a nursing home.

Dad worked hard all his life and had accumulated some $60,000. Not much money even by 1980 standards. His wife had nothing of her own, so he applied for Medicaid to cover the cost of her nursing care. He was told to reapply when he had "spent down" to $2,000.

That really bothered me. Why did he need to become impoverished because my step-mother needed nursing care? I guess I wasn't the only one that felt that way because congress passed the Medicare Catastrophic Coverage Act in 1988. The Medicaid section of that act remedied the situation by considering the assets of the couple as being part of a common pot and allowing the non-institutionalized spouse to keep his/her own share of that pot. Over the years, congress increased the maximum amount the spouse can keep up to the current (2004) value of $92,760.

Unfortunately, the way the law is written, states can opt for less than the federal maximum, provided the state allows the non-institutionalized spouse to keep at least the minimum value set by the federal government. That minimum is currently $18,552.

Even in those states that allow the federal maximum value, many people find themselves in my father's situation. They must spend down their life savings until they have no more than that allowed under the law.

Many people have chosen to divorce their spouse rather than spend down. I witnessed two such cases. One was in the nursing home that housed my step-mother. I met this elderly gentlemen. His mind was clear, but his body frail. He was unable to care for himself, so his wife placed him in this nursing home. She was an attractive, well-dressed woman. That he loved her was obvious. His eyes would light up as soon as she entered the door.

One day he told me that she wanted a divorce. He made all sorts of excuses for her "You know I had some money when we married, but not as much as her. She has a lot. We signed a pre-nuptial agree-ment saying that in the event we divorce, we part with whatever we came into the marriage. I didn't mind signing that agreement. This is a second marriage for both of us. She has two children and wanted to be sure they inherit her money. All I wanted was to be with her. The money meant noth-ing to me. "

"Now she wants a divorce. I can understand how she feels. Why should she spend all that money when I can qualify for Medicaid as soon as we divorce? It isn't like we will really be divorced. We still love each other. Nothing will change."

But it did. Her visits gradually tapered off. He would sit by the window waiting for her visit. Some days she would call saying that something came up and she'd have to come another time. Those days were hard for him. The sadness in his eyes filled my eyes as well.

He never did go on Medicaid. He used whatever money he had to pay for his nursing care over the next several months. He died before it was necessary for him to apply for Medicaid.

The second divorce case involved a devoted couple who were married for over thirty years when the wife was diagnosed with early stage Alzheimer's disease. They were upset to think that their hard earned savings would need to be spent on expensive nursing home care. They agreed to divorce to protect their savings.

I met the couple at the tennis court. He would play tennis a couple of days a week. His former wife would sit on the sidelines and watch him play. After the game, he would take her to lunch, and then home. That she had diminished capacity was obvious. Her eyes never left him. She would follow him wherever he went, much like a two year old following a parent around.

At lunch he would order for both of them. Some days he had to cut her food and help her eat. Eventually she was too ill to accompany him at tennis. But she continued to live with him. When she became bedridden, he hired a nurse to help care for her.

He never could bring himself to place her in a nursing home, so there was no reason to apply for Medicaid. She died with him by her side.

I don't know what bothered me more. The desperate measures people felt they must take or government policy. I wondered why the government didn't require people to be impoverished in order to qualify for a open heart surgery or expensive chemotherapy for those with cancer? Medicare pays hundreds of thousands of dollars per person for such treatment. Yet the government balks at paying for long term nursing care for those poor souls who are unable to care for themselves.

I decided there had to be a way to qualify for Medicaid other than divorce. That's when I began the study of Elder Law. I read all the laws relating to Medicaid. It turned out to be a daunting task. There are many levels of law that govern Medicaid. There are the federal statutes (Social Security Act Title XIX/P.L. 89-97); the U.S. Code of Federal Regulations (42 CFR 430-435) and the Centers for Medicare and Medicaid Services State Medicaid Manual, Part 3 that say how the federal statutes are to be administered in the United States.

There are state Medicaid statutes and the state administrative code that explain how the Medicaid program is administered within the state. In addition, most states provide a manual to caseworkers who take applications and determine eligibility. The manual tells how to determine whether the Applicant qualifies for Medical Assistance.

These six different layers of laws and regulations are constantly changing — often with little or no notice to the general public.

And the laws are not well written.
In *Rehabilitation Association of Virginia v. Kozlowski*, 4 2 F.3d 1444, 1450 (4th Cir 1994), the Court had nothing but sympathy for officials who must interpret or administer these laws. "There can be no doubting that the statutes and provisions in question, involving the financing of Medicare and Medicaid, are among the most completely impenetrable texts within human experience. Indeed, one approaches them . . . with dread, for not only are they dense reading of the most tortuous kind, but Congress also revisits the area frequently, generously cutting and pruning in the process and making any solid grasp of the matters addressed merely a passing phase."

That's legalese for "The Medicare and Medicaid laws are hard to understand and once you think you've got it, Congress changes the law."

But the fact that there are so many different, complex laws gave me an opportunity to "cross-ruff." I could use federal law to work out a strategy to reduce my client's assets to that allowed by state law. For example, federal law allows the person who is applying for Medicaid, or his spouse, to spend down their assets by purchasing an annuity, provided the annuity meets all of the requirements set by the federal government. I could advise a person who was over the maximum value to use that extra money to buy an annuity that conformed to federal statute. Once the annuity was purchased, the person could qualify for Medicaid in the given state.

I wish I could say that I was clever enough to think up the annuity and other strategies by myself, but that's not true. In 1991, I joined the National Academy of Elder Law Attorneys. They offer seminars in different parts of the country. Attorneys from all over the United States meet together to study the law and exchange ideas.

Within a few years I became very successful at getting my clients qualified for Medicaid. My efforts, and those of my fellow Elder Law attorneys, did not go unnoticed by the government. States began to challenge different strategies we were using. New laws were passed limiting some of our Medicaid qualifying plans. For example, several states now have laws that prevent the use of an annuity to qualify for Medicaid.

DIY IS THE WAY TO GO
IF YOU ARE QUALIFIED

There is no reason to employ an attorney if you are eligible for Medicaid. The state criteria for Medicaid eligibility is usually printed at the state's Medical Assistance web site. See the Public Information Section of Eagle Publishing Company for the Web site of your state Medical Assistance program. http://www.eaglepublishing.com

Most state web sites give a detailed explanation of what programs are available to those who are poor and disabled and how to apply. You can call or visit the agency that administers the Medicaid program for additional information.

There are many forms to complete in order to apply for Medical Assistance. There are people in the state agency that administers the program who will help you fill out the forms. The important thing is to be truthful. Whatever you say will be checked by the state. There are stiff penalties for those who are convicted of obtaining Medicaid benefits fraudulently. And there is no reason to do so. There are all sorts of legally permissible strategies to arrange the applicant's finances so that he will qualify for Medicaid within a relatively short period of time. That's what Elder Law attorneys do. They explain to the client what is allowed under state and federal law in order for the applicant to qualify for government benefits.

The only question that remains is whether to DIY or to employ an Elder Law attorney to help you (or your disabled family member) qualify for Medical Assistance.

DIY is difficult for those with too much in assets. State agencies are willing to share information about what Medical Assistance programs are available to those who are qualified. They will not offer information about which of the couple's assets count when applying for Medicaid and which are exempt. An experienced Elder Law attorney will be able to provide you with this information.

In addition to not saying which items are exempt, most state agencies will not tell the public what transactions will trigger disqualification and which transactions are permissible under state law. Some states such as Oregon publish the handbook used by the Medical Assistance workers to determine eligibility on the Internet. They seem to be genuinely interested in helping those in need.

But Oregon is the exception, not the rule. Most states are secretive. They publish nothing about how to qualify for Medicaid on the Internet. They instruct their workers not to offer any suggestion about how an Applicant might arrange his finances so he can qualify for Medical Assistance.

For those who are over the limit, at least one consultation with an Elder Law attorney is warranted.

The reader might be thinking that all Elder Law attorneys are Mr. Right because they help their client to get Medical Assistance. But going back to our Normal Curve, for every hundred Elder Law attorneys, expect a couple to be Mr. Wrong.

EXPERIENCE

Before employing an Elder Law attorney you need to know what percentage of his practice is devoted to Elder Law and how long he has been practicing in the field. Give him a plus if he is certified as an Elder Law attorney.

Few states have certification programs for Elder Law, however, the National Elder Law Foundation offers a certification program. To be certified by the National Elder Law Foundation, the attorney must have at least five years experience in Elder Law and must pass a certification exam.

Not being certified as an Elder Law attorney does not necessarily merit a minus. It takes time to study for the certification examination. And there is a healthy cost to take it. There are many competent, experienced attorneys who have not taken the time (and money) to become certified.

If the lawyer is not certified in Elder Law, ask whether he has taken courses in Elder Law and whether he attended any of the seminars offered by the National Academy of Elder Law Attorneys.

You will want to know whether he practices Elder Law on a full time basis. Practicing Elder Law is not a part-time thing. The attorney must keep up to date on all of the state and federal laws regulating the Medicaid program.

Most importantly, he needs to know how the Medicaid program is being administered in your county. The laws relating to Medicaid are so complex, that one county may interpret the law differently than the next. What might be an acceptable Medicaid qualifying strategy in one county, might be rejected in another county. The Elder Law attorney needs to know which county will accept the particular strategy he is suggesting.

He also needs to be knowledgeable and experienced about the appeal process in the event that your application is denied.

Once you are satisfied that he knows what he is doing, the next thing to consider is how much he is going to charge to get the Applicant onto Medicaid, and here's where you need to set up your defenses.

How To Defend Against
Your Elder Law Attorney

In most states, the "going price" for getting a person onto Medicaid is approximately equal to the cost of a one month stay in a nursing home. Generally, lawyers charge a flat fee and do not charge for costs. Some will ask for the full payment up front. Others will ask for half to get started and half when the application is filed. What you do not want to see is a lawyer who asks for a large retainer without investigating whether you have a problem in the first place.

It is reasonable for an Elder Law attorney to charge an initial consultation fee of a few hundred dollars. Your problem may be easily solved and he can make some suggestions that will enable you to apply for Medicaid on your own. It is not reasonable for him to charge thousands of dollars before he will agree to "take your case." If his receptionist indicates that this is his method of practicing Elder Law, find another attorney. If you find that he is the only Elder Law attorney in your area, do some investigation on your own before you decide that you need to employ him. Check to see whether there are Alzheimer's Association or Parkinson's support groups available in your area. These organizations offer a wealth of information to assist the families of those who are ill. Through these organizations, you may meet other people who used this attorney.

Having gone through the process, a former client can tell you what to expect when you apply for Medicaid. The former client can tell you whether the lawyer was instrumental in getting the applicant approved for Medicaid, or whether they could just as well have qualified on their own.

Will He Be There For You?

Each applicant, or a family member if he is too ill to apply, must appear in person for an interview before the agency that administers the state medical assistance program. The interview usually lasts an hour or two. The case worker will have you bring in much documentation such as the applicant's social security card, birth certificate or naturalization papers, etc. They will want to know everything that is owned by the applicant and his spouse — deeds, bank accounts, securities, insurance policies, etc.

It is comforting to have your attorney with you to help you understand the procedure and to assist you in the event that the case worker has some question about the application. Before you employ an Elder Law attorney you will want to know whether it is his practice to accompany the client to the interview.

Give him a plus, plus if he says "yes." Give him a plus if it is his practice to send an experienced legal assistant to accompany you. Give him a minus, if he indicates that you will be on your own.

Will He Give You A Choice?

There are those who do not enjoy thinking for themselves. When they go to a lawyer, it's just "Tell me what to do and I'll do it." They reason that the lawyer is a professional and knows what he is doing, so why insult him by asking questions.

Those who read the introduction to this book know I am not from that school. I believe the role of the lawyer needs to evolve to that of doctor. The lawyer needs to say "These are your options. These are the risks associated with those options. Now tell me what you want to do."

This approach is especially desirable in the field of Elder Law. As explained, Medicaid laws can change quickly and without warning. The strategy that your lawyer recommends may be good one day, but not the day you happen to apply.

An experienced lawyer knows this can happen. He should be willing to give you several options, along with his opinion about the probability that it will be challenged. Each person has his own comfort level when it comes to risks. You should be the one to decide whether you want to take a very conservative approach or whether you want to push the envelope.

In addition to giving you the choice of strategy, he should offer you a back-up plan in the event that the application is denied. It is better to put "Plan B" into effect, than to contest the denial.

Contesting the denial can be a lengthy procedure. Federal law requires the first step in the process be an administrative appeal called a "Fair Hearing." I always thought this expression to be government speak. In my opinion, there is nothing fair about a Fair Hearing. Federal law requires that the hearing officer be "impartial."

But the hearing officer is employed by, and serves at the pleasure of, the same state agency that denied the application. More likely than not, the hearing officer will support the state's position.

Should the application be denied at the Fair Hearing level, the applicant will need to take the next step in the appeal process. In most states, the next step is an appeal to the state court. If that fails the applicant can take his appeal to federal court, all the way up to the U.S. Supreme Court.

Before you decide upon a particular strategy, you should ask your attorney how much he will charge to represent you at the Fair Hearing in the event the application is denied. If he quotes you an hourly rate, then ask approximately how long it usually takes him to represent a client at the Fair Hearing. This will give you some idea of the cost of the first step in the appeals process. That knowledge may influence your choice of strategies.

Should an appeal be necessary, all the things we said about open-ended fee agreements apply. If he asks you to sign an hourly fee agreement, you should remind him of his estimated cost of appeal and then try to negotiate a fixed price fee agreement based on that estimate.

Personal Injury 10

We've all seen the ads that say "If you have been injured, call us. We charge no fee unless we recover money for you." What the ads are describing is the *contingency fee agreement*. The lawyer's pay is contingent on his ability to get money for his client. The lawyer gets a percentage of the *damages* (lawyer talk for monies recovered for the client). The contingency fee can run anywhere from 25% to 50%. Most commonly it is one-third of the damages. Although the lawyer's fee is contingent on winning, costs are another thing.

Costs are the out-of-pocket expenses incurred during the case. Expenses can be substantial in a Personal Injury ("P.I.") case. Doctors charge thousands of dollars to testify about how badly you have been hurt. Forensic scientists may need to be employed. In addition, you will need to pay for travel expenses, court reporter fees, long distance telephone calls, fax charges, postage, and on and on.

The laws of the state vary with regard to costs. To discourage *litigation* (law suits), some states require the client to pay costs. In such states, your attorney may require that you give him thousands of dollars to cover those costs. In states that do not require the client to pay costs, the lawyer will front expenses, but he will expect to be reimbursed when the case is settled. Either way, you will end up with a lot less than the percentage of the damages you expected.

Shopping for Mr. Right is easier in personal injury cases than in any other branch of law because competition in the field is so keen, yet you need to be wary of P.I. lawyers who are overly eager to sign you up.

HONESTY

Red flags should go up in the event that an attorney approaches you and says that he can get you a large settlement for the pain you have suffered. Solicitation, otherwise known as "ambulance chasing" is unprofessional conduct. In most states, an attorney who solicits clients can be de-barred for doing so. Many states allow lawyers to advertise in newspapers and even on television. However, lawyers are not allowed to directly approach a new client and offer legal services.

Those who have had a hard time finding work may be sympathetic with the lawyer who solicits business. But to employ such an attorney is risky. If he has no respect for the rules of his own profession, why should he respect your rights? And why does he feel he needs to solicit clients? Most new clients come from referrals from prior clients. Doesn't he have satisfied clients who will refer him?

If you are badly injured and are in the hospital, you may think the first thing to do is call a lawyer. Many will respond to such a request by visiting you in the hospital.

This may not be the best route to go. Choosing Mr. Right P.I. Lawyer might be the most important decision you make in you life. You should not make it unless you are up to it. Painkillers can dull the senses as well as your physical discomfort. The retainer agreement placed in front of you may be written in legalese. You need to be alert enough to fully understand the contract.

You also need to be well enough to travel to the lawyer's place of business to see what kind office he has. As we will see shortly, having a lawyer with a posh office, can impact the amount you receive at settlement.

Yet, as with the criminal case, it is important to employ a lawyer as quickly as possible after the injury so that he can collect and preserve evidence. For those who are severely injured, this presents a dilemma. You may be in the hospital for some time. In such case, have a family member or trusted friend help you line up Mr. Right.

A SOLE PRACTITIONER MAY NOT BE THE BEST CHOICE

Your search may not be so much for a lawyer, but rather a P.I. law firm. An attorney who practices law by himself may not have the time or resources to do justice to your case. If you decide to include a sole practitioner in your search, you need to ask how many other P.I. cases he is now handling, and whether he has another lawyer available to assist with research and court appearances.

If he is going to front the costs you need to be sure he has enough money to do so. It is easy to identify the lawyer with lots of money. His office is usually located on the top floor of an expensive office building. Marble floors, spacious conference room, works of art on the wall, a well dressed and solicitous receptionist, asking you whether you wish a cup of coffee or a soft drink — yes, wealth is not difficult to spot.

And neither is it difficult to spot the struggling lawyer. Instead of receptionist, he may have an answering service. His office may be in a fine looking office building, but he may be renting a one room office with shared office facilities either from the building manager or from another lawyer.

In Personal Injury law, success counts. You want the person you employ to have a good track record; and a wealthy lawyer is an indication of that success.

THE SUCCESSFUL P.I. FIRM
Identifying the top P.I. law firm may take some effort on your part. It isn't always the law firm with the biggest advertising budget. Those firms are seeking volume. They try to line up as many cases as possible with the intent to settle them quickly and without going to trial.

You may think these are admirable goals, however, too often the law firm will settle a solid case rather than take it to trial and get top dollar. It takes time and effort to bring the case to trial.

In the long run the firm makes more money by settling for a lesser sum and taking only a very small percentage of their case load to trial.

The best P.I. firm in town may be one that doesn't advertise at all. They get all the business they can handle by referrals from satisfied clients and other lawyers. If you know a lawyer, you can ask him to refer you to a top law firm. He will probably get a referral fee, but it should come out of the percentage earned by the P.I. firm and not from you. Because of this referral fee your attorney may be motivated to send you to the law firm who will get you the biggest award.

If you do not know an attorney, you might ask your local Bar Association if they can refer you to a large P.I. law firm in your area. Very often the best P.I. firm is the largest firm, but best usually means "has the most money."

You'll want to employ the best law firm in town for several reasons:

★   THEY HAVE MONEY TO FRONT COSTS
Having a lot of money puts a law firm in a position of power. They can spend as much as it takes to collect enough evidence to win. A smaller law firm may be forced to settle for less because it doesn't have enough time, staff, and money to go to trial.

★   THEY ONLY TAKE GOOD CASES

If a large law firm will take your case, it tells you that you have a good case and should win a substantial sum of money.

★   THEIR REPUTATION PRECEDES THEM

A large prestigious firm is intimidating to the opposing side. In a P.I. case the opposing side is often the company who insured the person who caused the harm. Insurance companies have top lawyers who know and respect other top P.I. lawyers. They know successful firms can afford to bypass lesser cases and take only solid cases. The opposing side is more likely to settle with a large law firm because they know that the case is good and the law firm has the resources to pursue it.

The treatment given to a smaller firm is very different. They generally give the smaller law firm or sole practitioner a "hard time." Their strategy is to wear down the small law firm by forcing him to argue every little legal point in court. This is expensive to the small law firm because it uses the time and energy of the few lawyers in the firm to prepare for, and attend, a court hearing.

Insurance attorneys often "stone-wall" a smaller firm by being uncooperative and refusing to discuss a settlement. If they decide your case is not strong, they will force it to trial. Trials cost a lot of money. Your case may be lost just because it is under funded.

You may be convinced that the top firm is the only firm for you, but you may never see the inside of the office because larger firms usually have a preliminary screening procedure. A legal assistant or attorney might call for the details of your case. Instead of making an appointment for you to come in and meet an attorney, you might get a letter saying "We are unable to take your case at this time, however this does not mean that your case is without merit. We encourage you to seek consultation with other law firms."

TRANSLATION: This is going to take more time, effort and money to pursue than the case is worth to us.

Don't be discouraged if you are turned down by the top P.I. firm, a medium size firm can give you good representation.

Before employing a law firm you will want to know how many lawyers are employed by the firm and the size of their supporting staff (legal assistants, clerks, receptionists, etc.). This will give you some idea of whether the firm has sufficient resources to bring your case to trial in the event it is necessary to do so.

Once you decide upon a law firm, you need to ask who in the firm will be doing the pretrial work in your case, and who will take it to trial.

Hopefully, that will be the same person. But many firms have one experienced trial attorney who does all of their trial work. Other lawyers in the firm do the pretrial work and only assist at trial.

This is not necessarily a bad arrangement, however you want to be aware of what to expect should you go to trial.

Most importantly, you need to get some idea of the value of your case. Experienced P.I. lawyers know the approximate value of a broken bone, a lost limb, or a wrongful death. True, these values can be more or less, depending on the circumstances of the case, but the P.I. attorney has a rough idea of what you will come away with, and he should share that knowledge with you.

It is important that you have some concept of the value of the case, because at some point in time, the other side will make an offer, and you need to know whether that offer is reasonable.

MEDIATION
Usually the first time an offer is made is at mediation. Mediation is an informal means of settling a dispute. The person conducting the mediation (the *mediator*) is a neutral party. He has no power to decide the matter. He is there just to help the parties come to an agreement.

Most judges will require that, prior to trial, the parties and their attorneys sit down with a mediator and try to settle the case.

THE RULES OF MEDIATION

1.   The mediator is impartial.

2.   Whatever is said during the mediation cannot be played back to you at trial.

These rules seem simple enough. But you can expect all sorts of games that will distress and annoy you; and in the worst case scenario, make you settle for much less than you should have.

Let's start with the choice of mediator.
The mediator is usually a person with a legal background or with special training in mediation. It is a favorite part-time occupation for retired judges. It is a way of earning extra income for struggling lawyers.

Some counties have a mediation training program available. People who fulfill the educational requirements are given a certificate saying they are qualified to work as a mediator within the state. In most of these programs, a law degree is desirable, but not necessary. What is required is training in the art of negotiation, because it is the job of the mediator to move the parties to a settlement that is acceptable to all parties.

PICKING THE RIGHT MAN FOR THE JOB

Mediators are usually paid by the hour. Some mediators charge by the job. Each party is required to pay half of the mediator's fee, so each party must agree to the choice of mediator.

Experienced attorneys know who is available from the mediator pool. Opposing attorneys usually agree between themselves who should serve as mediator. Some attorneys will choose mediators that they have worked with before with favorable results. The mediators, consciously or unconsciously will want to please attorneys who send lots of work their way. That's fine if your attorney has worked with the mediator many times in the past. Not so fine if your attorney doesn't know him, but the opposing counsel does.

Another important consideration is the legal background of the mediator. Some attorneys feel that they have a weak case and will choose a mediator who is a retired judge, or one with a respected legal background, hoping the mediator will be able to convince their client to settle the case and not go to trial.

The choice of mediator may make the difference between settling and not settling. This is one decision that you want to be in on from the beginning. You are the one who has to interface with the mediator. You should be the one who has the final say as to who that mediator should be.

Questions to ask your lawyer BEFORE he agrees to a choice of mediator:

- *How many times have you worked with this mediator ?*

- *What is the legal background of the mediator?*

- *Did you suggest this mediator or did the other attorney pick him?*

If you feel strongly that the other attorney is trying to get a mediator who will favor their case, or if your lawyer is trying to convince you not to go to trial and wants a retired judge as mediator, then you need to refuse that mediator.

There is no point asking the two lawyers to go back to the mediator pool. The opposing lawyer will still try to choose someone who will support his cause. If your lawyer is trying to get you to settle, he will pick still another mediator who will try to convince you that you have a weak case.

In such situations, you can take your chances with the court. When lawyers (or their clients) cannot agree on a mediator, they can ask the court to appoint someone for the job. You can direct your lawyer to ask the court for such an appointment. Pot luck beats a stacked deck.

Who Wants Most To Settle At Mediation?

If you answered "The lawyers," you're getting the hang of this game.

Your attorney is working on a contingency. He gets nothing if he loses. If he put money out for costs, his money is at stake as well. The defending attorney is probably working at an hourly rate but he's not anxious to go to trial either. He may not have his own money at stake, but if he loses, he's going to have one unhappy client, and that may impact his future employment.

The only certainty with a trial is that someone is going to lose. Each knows that the other side has a reasonable argument, else the parties wouldn't be taking it to trial in the first place. And they each know that going to court is a crap shoot. If there is one thing we all learned from the O. J. Simpson trial is that anything can happen during the trial. No one can truly predict how things are going to turn out.

In addition to the financial risk of losing, there is the blow to pride and reputation of the losing attorney. Who wins and who loses get around the court house pretty quick.

Yup, if there is one thing neither lawyer wants to do is go to trial.

The next in line to want a settlement is the mediator. It is his job to get the parties to come to an agreement. Coming away with a negotiated settlement is an "atta boy" for him. Coming away with an impasse does nothing to enhance his reputation. Neither lawyer will be happy about going to trial. They might decide to chose another mediator in the future.

Finally we get to the parties themselves. And if you hadn't noticed, they are least interested in settling.

True, the parties are not all that thrilled about going to trial. If you look up the word TRIAL in Roget's Thesaurus you will see words like "examination, law suit, difficulty, trouble, affliction, suffering, punishment." That doesn't sound like something anyone would willingly submit to.

So the parties might also be inclined to settle. But at what price?

That's the question Amanda and Bill had to ask themselves when they attended mediation. They lived in quiet rural community with winding roads that were ideal for walking and bicycle riding. Bill was the athletic type. Unfortunately, Amanda was the most uncoordinated person he ever met. She couldn't roller skate, ice skate or even ride a bike. There were few sports they could enjoy together until Bill got the idea of buying a tandem bicycle.

He rode the front of the bike with his wife behind him. Even with Bill steering, it took Amanda sometime to learn how to ride. Bill had to explain that she needed to peddle round — not square. "Amanda, your foot needs to go round in a circle. You're peddling as if your foot were following the outline of a box."

Finally she got the hang of it and they were able to bicycle together around the neighborhood. But they soon ran into trouble. One of their neighbors was an elderly man whose only companions were his pets. As they bicycled past his house, one of his dogs chased them, barking and growling.

When they got home, Bill called his neighbor and complained about the dog. The neighbor said the dog was a good dog. He was just playing and meant no harm. He assured Bill that the dog had never bitten anyone.

The next week, Bill and Amanda went biking again. This time there were two dogs on their neighbor's property. They came charging out, barking loudly. Bill and Amanda sped up trying to get away, but one dog jumped up knocking Bill off the bike. Amanda tried to kick the other dog, but he got her in the back of her foot in her Achilles tendon.

Bill hit his head on a rock when he fell off the bike and was knocked out cold. Amanda screamed in pain and fear. The old man heard the barking and screaming. He came out and chased the dogs off.

The dog's bite severed tendons in Amanda's foot. She had to undergo surgery to repair the damage. She went through weeks of physical therapy, but the doctors said that she might always walk with a limp.

Not only was Amanda hurt physically, but emotionally as well. The attack traumatized her. She had terrible nightmares about being attacked by animals. She became afraid of dogs and wouldn't visit any friend or family member who owned one.

Bill didn't fare much better. The concussion he suffered left him with migraine headaches.

After a few months, Bill and Amanda decided to sue and employed Carl as their lawyer. He said they had an excellent case because they both suffered permanent damage. It might be worth as much as a million dollars. Carl offered them a retainer agreement that required them to pay $10,000 to cover costs.

"We don't have that kind of money. We can barely keep up with our medical bills."

Carl said he would front the costs, but they had to agree to reimburse him from the settlement; which they readily did.

Carl filed the law suit against the neighbor. His homeowner's policy covered dog bites, so the insurance company had one of their lawyers defend the action. The insurance lawyer was most thorough in preparing his case. He got all of the couple's medical records, not only that of the attack but records of every other time they ever visited a doctor. He had them examined by his choice of doctors and psychiatrists.

Carl conducted his own investigation. He discovered that other neighbors had complained about the dogs. He wanted to have the dogs examined by a veterinarian; but the old man had them "put to sleep" shortly after the "accident."

Finally after several months of legal tap-dancing, Carl asked the court to set the matter for trial. As was the custom in that court, the judge required the parties to attend mediation before he would set a trial date.

At the beginning of mediation, each side presented their best argument to the mediator.

Carl explained how much his clients had suffered because of this vicious attack. He said the neighbor was negligent because he did not keep his dogs penned up after he had been warned by several people that they were dangerous.

The insurance attorney said neither dog had ever bitten anyone before. All the neighbors were complaining about was their barking. He said if Bill and Amanda thought the dog was dangerous, they shouldn't have ridden past the house. In fact, he intended to prove at trial that they deliberately rode past the house just to torment the dogs.

As for their injuries, he discovered that Bill had suffered a concussion while playing high school football. He complained about headaches then too. Probably his headaches were a result of that football injury. Besides the CAT scan did not show any brain damage.

He said Amanda was a nervous person and taking Prozac before the accident. Her fears and nightmares had nothing to do with the "accident." As for her foot, the insurance company doctor would testify that with time and physical therapy she should be walking just fine.

Amanda was furious "And who is going to pay for that therapy?"

The insurance lawyer said "As a good will gesture, we offer $50,000. That is more than generous."

Bill got up and said "We'll see you in court."

The mediator jumped up and said "Now let's not be hasty. I'm going to ask the plaintiffs to step into the next room while I discuss this with the defendants."

Once they were in a private room Amanda and Bill let their lawyer know just how upset they were with him. Bill said "How could you let him get away with saying we wanted to torment the dog? I called my neighbor. He assured me that the dog was only playing and would never hurt anyone. I believed him."

Amanda said, "What does the fact that I was taking Prozac have to do with the terrible nightmares I suffer night after night? That dog bite was terrible and vicious. That attack would give anyone night-mares. And I don't care what their doctor says about my foot. My doctor says I will never be able to walk without a limp."

Bill was equally adamant "I haven't suffered head-aches since my high school days. Now I have them all the time. "

Carl explained that the $50,000 was just a beginning number and that he was sure he could get a better offer.

The mediator came into the room and explained that he was able to convince the insurance attorney to increase his offer to $75,000.

Bill told the mediator what the lawyer could do with his $75,000.

The mediator said "Now hold on. The judge ordered you to mediation. If you won't at least make some sort of counter-offer, I will tell the judge that you refused to mediate in good faith. The judge could order sanctions against you."

"What does that mean?"

Carl explained that it meant the judge could order them to pay the other attorney for his time in attending this mediation.

"You mean the judge could fine me because I wouldn't agree to accept a terrible offer? I don't believe that."

Carl said "Just give him a reasonable counter offer to show the judge that we are trying to settle."

Bill said "O.K. Let's start with the million dollars you said the case was worth."

The mediation went back and forth like this for hours. At one point, Carl threatened to quit. "You don't understand, we can't win. They have all of your medical records. They have all kinds doctors and experts that will testify against you. If you won't agree to settle, I'm going to have to resign as your lawyer. I can't afford to go to trial knowing that we can't win."

Carl's wife could see that he was bone tired at the end of the day.

"How did it go?"

"We settled, but it was a long day."

"What'd you settle for?"

"$100,000."

"Is that all? I thought the case was worth more than that."

"Probably, but I couldn't take the risk. I just lost that drowning case, and took a terrible hit. I had over $50,000 of my own money in that case. I even borrowed to take it to trial. I'm in debt up to my eye-balls. I need the money. I had no choice but to settle."

THE LAW SUIT
THE GREATEST DANGER OF ALL

11

I believe it was the French philosopher Jean Jacques Rousseau who said that he had been involved in two law suits during his life. One he won and the other he lost. Both were equally painful to him. He observed that winning didn't make the experience any less painful than losing.

Make no mistake, litigation always involves high emotion. If not at the start, then surely as it progresses. If you decide to sue, more than likely it's because you are angry at the way you have been treated. If you are the one being sued, you will probably be angry at the other person's greed. In many cases, the emotion continues long after the case is settled.

What is surprising to those who venture into the litigation battle field is that all the enemies may not be on "the other side." As in war, you may find yourself exposed to "friendly fire." In this chapter, we hope to alert the reader to such dangers and to explain how to defend yourself from such attack.

FINDING MR. RIGHT

There is a popular misconception that a good *litigator* (trial attorney) must have an aggressive personality. Even other attorneys perpetrate the myth. That was the case when a business client of a large law firm asked whether the firm had lawyers who specialize in litigation. The attorney answered "Yes, we do. We keep them in a locked room at the end of the hallway. Once a day we throw them some raw meat."

But if you are looking for a pugnacious guy with a short fuse, you are looking for the wrong guy. A litigator needs to work smoothly within the court system. He must be able to interface with clerks, judges and yes, even the opposing attorney. You want to employ an attorney with good social skills. You will also want someone who has an air of self-confidence. Trial work is stressful. You need someone who can handle that stress. A trial attorney who is nervous or insecure, is in the wrong line of work.

Although self-confidence is desirable in a litigator, its extreme is not. You do not want to employ an attorney who seems pompous or arrogant. Your lawyer may need to convince a jury of the merit of your case. Arrogance is not an endearing feature. You want the jurors to like the person you chose to present your side of the story.

THE RETAINER AGREEMENT

All the things we said about employing an experienced and successful trial lawyer in the last chapter still applies. The only problem is that you may not have much of a choice. While there are any number of lawyers willing to take a Personal Injury case on contingency, few will agree to take the risk with other types of law suits. They will want an hourly fee to defend you if you are sued, and an hourly fee to sue someone on your behalf.

There a few exceptions. Lawyers who do guardianship** litigation may consider representing a client without demanding a retainer of thousands of dollars, if the lawyer is reasonably certain that the court will order his fees be paid from the monies of the ward (the incapacitated person).

Guardianship is an area of law that is increasingly a subject of litigation. As our population ages, the number of guardianships increases. The older a person gets, the greater the probability he will need someone to help care for his person and his property. That should not be a problem for the person who made provision for someone to take over in the event of his incapacity. If he did not have the forethought to make such provision and he cannot care for himself, the court will step in and appoint a guardian of his person to see that his physical needs are met; and a guardian to care for his property.

** In some states, it's called conservatorship.

In most cases, the court appoints the same person to serve as guardian of the ward's person and property, but not in Sidney's case. Sidney was a wealthy business man. He was an "in control" kind of guy. He was most generous with his daughter from his first marriage, and with Debbie, his second wife. He gave them everything they wanted, except control over his money. Neither had access to his bank accounts or property. Everything he owned was in his name only.

This arrangement worked fine while Sidney was capable of handling his affairs, but one day he had a massive stroke. The doctors were able to save his life, but the stroke left him paralyzed and semi-conscious. They tried treatment and physical therapy for several weeks, but eventually there was nothing more they could do. The doctors told Debbie they were going to discharge him from the hospital.

"I can't care for him at home in this condition."

"There is a nursing home near by that will give him the 24 hour care he needs. The admissions director will help you make arrangements to have him transferred there."

Debbie had to fill out a battery of papers when she applied for her husband's admission. Luckily, she was in the habit of carefully reading everything before she signed it. Buried deep in the admissions package was a statement that she agreed to be personally responsible to pay for her husband's care.

"I'm not going to pay for his care. He has his own money."

"But he can't sign a check. Don't you have a joint account or his Power of Attorney."

"No, he took care of everything."

"In that case, you will need to go to court and ask the judge to appoint you as his guardian."

"How do I do that?"

"You need to hire a lawyer to help you. I can refer you to several lawyers in the area who are experienced in guardianship matters."

Debbie went to the lawyer's office that same day. He asked for a retainer of $2,000.

"No. Why do I need to spend my money because he needs a guardian?"

"O.K. I'll take the case, and ask the court to be paid from your husbands assets."

Little did the lawyer or Debbie know that at the same time, Sidney's daughter was visiting her own lawyer.

"I want to take care of my father. He's been married to Debbie for only a few months. She doesn't know what's best for him."

Her lawyer explained "In this state, the spouse has top priority when it comes to being appointed as guardian."

"I'm not going to let her be in charge of my father. She doesn't care for him. She only married him for his money."

"I'll take your case, but my fee is $250 an hour plus costs and I will need a retainer of $5,000. If the court appoints you as his guardian, your attorney fees will be paid from your father's assets. But if you lose, the money you spent in fighting this case will come out of your own pocket."

The court battle was lengthy, expensive and bitter. Each side accused the other of only being interested in managing Sidney's substantial wealth.

The judge made a King Solomon-like decision to divide the guardianship in half. He made the daughter the guardian of Sidney's person and his wife the guardian of his property.

It was a good thing Sidney was comatose. He would have had a heart attack if he knew that he paid for both sides of the argument over who should be his guardian. Because the court appointed both the daughter and the wife as guardian, they each were entitled to be reimbursed for their attorney fees. The court awarded over $100,000 to the two opposing lawyers.

You might think is this the end of the story, but it gets worse. Within weeks, spouse and daughter were at it again.

The daughter did not like the nursing home Debbie had chosen.

"My father is a wealthy man. He deserves to be cared in a better place than this dump."

"There's nothing wrong with this nursing home. He's well cared for. Why spend money on a fancy place when he doesn't even know where he is?"

"I'm the guardian of his person and I say he goes to the nursing home of my choice."

"Well, I'm the guardian of his property and I won't pay for it!"

Back to court they went. But the judge had it with both of them. He discharged each of them as guardian. He appointed a trust company to manage Sidney's property and a professional guardian to serve as the guardian of his person.

And, yes. He awarded attorney's fees for the daughter, the spouse, the trust company and the professional guardian — all to be paid from Sidney's assets, of course.

The moral of that story is to avoid the need to have a guardian appointed in the first place, else you might find yourself in the ridiculous position of paying one lawyer to argue for the appointment of your guardian and another lawyer to argue against the appointment.

Avoiding guardianship is such an important topic, that I am in the process of writing a separate book on the subject. But for now, let us return to the subject of this chapter, namely

How To Defend Against Your Trial Lawyer

LOYALTY

In the first chapter we said that loyalty was the most important quality in a lawyer. We discussed loyalty in the context of conflict of interest between what is best for the client, and what is the most profitable to the lawyer. That is a major concern in litigation. It's easy for a lawyer to "make work" when fighting a law suit. The lawyer can decide he needs to research every point of law. He can decide he needs to "toe to toe" every single disagreement with the opposing lawyer rather than try to work something out without the need to bring the issue before the court.

This is similar to the illegal practice of "churning" a stock brokerage account. The stockbroker decides to buy and sell, not as part of a plan to maximize his client's investment, but rather to generate commission for himself.

The example given in Chapter 4, of Barbara, the divorce lawyer, going to court rather than reschedule a deposition, can be considered as churning the account.

She billed her client for several hours of work:
- $$ researching whether Robert had the right to bring a Motion for Protective Order

- $$ preparing her opening and closing argument for the hearing

In addition, she charged travel expenses to go to the court and for the cost of getting a transcript of the hearing. Her client paid well over a $1,000 and received no benefit in return.

To defend yourself against churning, you need to tell your lawyer, up front, that you will expect him to give you a copy of everything that is filed in the case. You will want to require him to tell you whenever he plans to go to court and the reason that he thinks it is necessary to do so.

Had Barbara's client required a copy of everything that was filed, she would have seen Robert's Motion For Protective Order. She could have told Barbara to work out the problem and not to waste Barbara's time and the client's money by going to court to argue the point.

Another way to discourage churning is to make sure the lawyer has a stake in the action. If he is on a contingency fee, he gets a percentage of what ever money is recovered. He makes the same percentage whether he spends lots of time at court or not. He makes the most money by settling the matter as quickly as possible and spending as little of his time as possible on the case.

You can turn an hourly rate into a contingency fee by offering to pay the lawyer a lower hourly rate in exchange for a percentage of the recovery. Suppose your lawyer wants $300 an hour to sue on your behalf. You might offer $200 an hour and 25% of the monies you win. Your retainer agreement should say that all of the monies you paid will be credited toward that 25%. For example, if you win $100,000 he is entitled to $25,000, but if you already paid $10,000, he will receive the difference of $15,000.

This modified contingency arrangement should discourage the lawyer from generating unnecessary fees and costs.

FRIENDLY ENEMIES
Loyalty also relates to having your lawyer put your interest above his personal or professional relationship with other lawyers. You may think it a given that your lawyer will consider the opposing lawyer to be his enemy. That's not usually the case.

They are more like wrestlers who battle each other to the ground. They expect to win sometimes and lose others. The experienced litigator knows and accepts the risks. The trial lawyer's mantra is "Sometimes I get the bear, and sometimes the bear gets me."

If your lawyer and the opposing counsel have practiced in the same county for a number of years, more than likely, they know and are friendly with each other. They probably socialize at Bar functions. They may refer clients back and forth to each other. That friendship can get in the way of your case. I learned that from personal experience.

I was involved in a law suit and had just employed an attorney to represent me. He called one day and said, "I ran into one of the lawyers who works in the firm of the opposing counsel. He told me that the girl we just hired as a part-time typist works full time at their firm."

"Didn't you ask her where she worked before you hired her?"

"I don't know if anyone asked her that question. Our office manager hired her to do some typing on week-ends."

"You mean she works unsupervised?"

"Yes, we leave her the work and she does it."

"But that leaves my files unprotected. She could go back and tell the opposing counsel everything about my case."

"Oh, she wouldn't do that; and even if she did, I know he would refuse to listen."

I couldn't believe what I was hearing. My lawyer had to be the most naive person I ever met, or a simpleton devoid of all common sense. If he was such good buddies with the opposing counsel, why didn't his buddy lawyer tell about the secretary instead of being tipped off by another member of the law firm?

Did it ever occur to my lawyer that maybe that member of the firm was trying to tell him something?

Why was a full-time secretary seeking part-time work in another firm? The law firm of the opposing counsel was a large, busy law firm. Surely they could have given her over-time if she needed extra money.

I wanted to fire him on the spot. But I didn't. He took the case on a contingency basis. I had interviewed two other top attorneys in town. Both turned me down. If I fired him, I would have had to employ an out-of-town lawyer, or a lawyer with a lesser reputation. Being pragmatic, I asked him to keep my files in a separate locked cabinet with no one having access to the key except him and his own personal secretary. He agreed, but he made me feel as if it were an imposition.

His secretary understood my concern. She offered to put a security code on my computer files. No one but she and my lawyer would be able to access my files.

But the damage to our attorney-client relationship was irreparable. I felt I could no longer trust him. His actions showed me where his loyalties were. First place was his friend, the opposing counsel. Second place was the part-time secretary who he just employed. I came in third place, if at all.

I expected that when we went into mediation, he would lean on me hard to settle rather than go to trial against his buddy. I was not disappointed.

Luckily I was prepared, and if you ever need to go into mediation, you need to be too.

How To Defend Yourself
Against Your Lawyer At Mediation

Mediation is a critical point in the law suit. How your attorney conducts himself may be directly related to your fee agreement. If he is working strictly by the hour, he will not be inclined to settle for much less than he thinks the case is worth. He will be ready and willing to go to trial unless he truly believes that he cannot win. In such case he will encourage you to settle. Sure he can make money by going to trial, but his reputation suffers with every loss.

The lawyer who is working on a contingency basis will try to talk you into settling. But there are three ways you can defend against high pressure tactics.

FIRST, DEMAND A PRE-MEDIATION CONFERENCE.
Many lawyers will schedule a pre-mediation conference with their client so that they can discuss the strategy they intend to use at the mediation. If your lawyer doesn't suggest an in person pre-mediation conference you should insist on having one. At the conference you should ask:
"Do you think we should settle?"

This is almost a silly question. Of course he thinks you should settle. But it is better to let him think you are agreeable to any offer.

Once he says he thinks you should settle your next question should be "Why?" Let him tell you all of the reasons you can't win. Better to know his position before going into the conference.

There is no point in telling him all of the reasons you think you should win. He knows all of the strong points of your case. Save all of your arguments in support of your case for mediation.

Once he explains all the reasons he thinks you should settle, the next question to ask is "For how much?" Expect a low-ball answer. His job will be easier if you are willing to settle for less than he thinks the other side will offer. If he gets more than that value, he will expect you to be most grateful.

SECOND, DO NOT GIVE HIM YOUR POSITION.

Be non-committal at the pre-mediation conference. Exposing your position to your lawyer will only be to your detriment. If you tell him you intend to settle, he will know it is only a question of how much. He will want to know what number you had in mind. You'd be wise not to give any dollar value. Those of you who are in the business world know that experienced negotiators start with a high "going in" position. The negotiator doesn't expect to get that value, its just a starting point. It is not the end point.

If you give him the amount you intend to settle for, he might take it as your going in position and you will ultimately end up with much less. If you give him your true "going in" figure, he may get upset with you and accuse you of being unrealistic.

Best that you do not say anything about how much you will accept to settle. Better yet, make no mention of whether you intend to settle or go to trial.

Remember at this pre-mediation conference, you want to get your lawyer's position. You want to know what part of the case is bothering him. You will want to know what number he had in mind. Your goal should be to get information, and not to give any. However, if he indicates that he wants to settle for significantly less than is acceptable, you need to let him know, in no uncertain terms, that his starting number needs to be a whole lot higher.

THIRD, EXPECT SOME ROUGH TREATMENT.

Those who read the last chapter may think that the lawyer's behavior at mediation was a result of his basic dishonesty, and that the average litigator doesn't act in that manner, but the tactics Carl used are very common. The only difference between Carl and the honest litigator is that he insisted on settling for considerably less than the case was worth.

If your lawyer is working on a contingency basis, he will be more motivated to settle than you are. Expect him to use every argument he can think of to convince you to settle. The most common one is *"You can't win!"*

The problem with this statement is that it might be true.

That was the case with Barbara, the divorce law. She knew that there was no way she could win the case. That was not the case with Carl, the Personal Injury lawyer of the last Chapter. He had a good case but was afraid to go to trial because of his own finances. The way to protect yourself from the Carls of the world is to have a good idea of the value of the case before you employ a lawyer. You can get that estimate by asking each of the three lawyers you interview how much they think your case is worth. Then use your own common sense to decide whether the information gathered by both sides during the course of litigation significantly changes that value.

"You must settle, or the judge will fine you."
This argument is rarely used because it is just pure bull. The judge might fine you if you do not attend the mediation after being ordered to do so. He also might consider a fine if you stone-wall and make absolutely no attempt at trying to negotiate a settlement. However, you cannot be fined just because the offer made is unacceptable to you.

"I'm going to quit!"
Again, this is one of those statements that might be true. You need to be prepared to have your lawyer walk away from the case. If he does, you will need to employ a new lawyer to go to trial. But if your lawyer is working on contingency, more than likely this threat is a bluff. He has put in considerable time and effort on your case. If he walks away, it will probably be a total loss for him. If he stays and goes to trial, he still has a chance at winning.

Had Carl's client refused to settle, more than likely he would have taken the case to trial. And it may not have been necessary to do so. If they refused to settle at mediation, the insurance lawyer may have been impressed with the client's confidence in their case, and decided to come back with a more realistic offer before going to trial.

THE DIY LAWSUIT 12

People worry about being sued should they happen to be in a car accident. The best way to protect against being sued is to purchase sufficient car insurance. Those who are poor can afford to be insured for the lowest amount under the law. They should not fear being sued because lawyers are not interested in suing if there is no way to collect the judgment. Attorneys are not about to spend their time, effort and money unless there is a pot of gold they can tap into.

If you are the *plaintiff* (the one who has been harmed) and the other party (the *defendant*) is insured, his insurance company will send in a skilled lawyer to defend him. You can expect the insurance company attorney to be smart, experienced, diligent and un-sympathetic to your cause.

A plaintiff who has a lawyer doesn't deal directly with the insurance company. He leaves negotiation to his attorney. But insurance lawyers are masters of intimidation, and will try to convince your lawyer (and you) that there is no way you can win. One method commonly used is to put up a good front. The insurance attorney may dress in expensive clothes. He may require you to come to his office to take a deposition so that you will be impressed with his expensive office. He is hoping that you will think that your lawyer couldn't possibly win against such a high powered law firm.

The problem is compounded when the plaintiff senses that his own lawyer does not want to go to trial. As explained in Chapter 10, the lawyer's reluctance may have nothing to do with the strength of the case. After reading that story you may be thinking that Bill and Amanda would have been better off without Carl. But self-representation has its pitfalls.

THE DIY PLAINTIFF

Insurance lawyers must have trouble containing their glee when a person who has been injured says he is not represented by counsel. It's like running a one horse race. The insurance lawyer can't lose. The worse that can happen is that the injured party refuses to settle and gets himself a lawyer. And all that will do is take the insurance lawyer and the plaintiff back to the position they would have been in the first place. Meanwhile time has passed, and what all good insurance lawyers know is that the more time passes, the better it is for them. It may be difficult for the plaintiff's attorney to collect evidence once weeks or months have passed.

Without an opposing attorney, the insurance company can concentrate on negotiating a settlement. They will send in an experienced adjuster to work at establishing good relations. The adjuster may appear solicitous, and interested in helping the injured party. But don't be deceived, it is his job to get the injured party to settle for as little as possible.

The adjuster will want to learn as much as he can about the injured party, his family, his job — anything that will tell him which button to push to make that person want to settle.

Adjusters are most successful with those who seek instant gratification — those impatient souls who want the money NOW. They are not willing to take the time to employ a lawyer who will try to get top dollar. They figure that if they settle directly (and quickly) with the insurance company they will ultimately end up with the same amount of money because there will not be any lawyer to pay (or get in the way).

That may be true, but the problem is that the injured person does not know how much his case is worth, and the adjuster is not about to tell him. He will tell him how much money the company is willing to settle for. The amount he quotes will be the company's lowest offer.

The injured person may think he can negotiate the price, but he is at a disadvantage. The adjuster knows the injured person is in a hurry to get his money and will use that fact against him. The usual ploy is "Look, if you will settle for this sum, I can get the check to you within the week."

Before accepting the offer the injured person would do well to check with different Personal Injury lawyers until he gets at least three estimates of the value of his case. He should take the average value of the estimates and then subtract away the lawyer's fee. That number is the amount he should aim for in his negotiations with the insurance company.

That value is fair for the injured person and for the insurance company as well. The company knows that a lawyer for the injured person will want at least 25% more than that value to cover his own attorney fees. The insurance company can afford to agree to settle on that value not only because it is a low settlement amount but also because of the money they save on their own attorney fees.

THE SMALL CLAIM

A person who wishes to sue someone for a small amount of money can usually file a small claim without the assistance of a lawyer. All states have a small claims court. The maximum value that can be pursued in a small claims court varies from state to state. If you wish to sue someone, call the clerk of the small claims court and ask the top value. If the amount of your loss is less than that value, you can pursue the case on your own.

Many courts print booklets that explain how to file a small claim. Small claim procedures are relatively simple to follow. The court usually orders the parties to attend mediation before setting the matter for trial. Mediation will give you some idea of the strength or weakness of your case. If you don't come to an agreement at mediation, you will need to present your case to the court for settlement.

The key is to winning at trial is to be prepared. Have as much hard evidence as possible. Instead of telling the judge "I gave him $3,000 to paint my house, but he didn't do the trim," it's better to have the cancelled check showing that you paid the money.

You also need to demonstrate to the court that both you and the painter understood that the price quoted included the trim.

If you tell the judge "We agreed that the $3,000 was to paint the whole house, including the trim" you are describing an oral contract. There's a legal joke that goes "oral contracts are not worth the paper they are written on."

Expect the judge to be skeptical about an oral agreement. To win your case you will need a witness who can verifying that you both agreed that the price included the trim, or you might win if you are able to demonstrate that the going price to paint a house, trim and all, is $3,000.

It's one thing to have the judge rule in your favor, but collecting the amount awarded to you is another matter. There are still other procedures for collecting money judgments. Those procedures are often more complicated than getting the judgment itself. If your painter resists giving you the money, you still may need to employ a lawyer to enforce the court order.

PATENTS   13
THE STUFF OF DREAMS

No doubt about it, Maggie was a dreamer. As a teenager she dreamed about becoming a famous country singer. That never happened. She dreamed of growing up and having a happy marriage. Two husbands and three children later she gave up on that dream.

Her life was a drudgery. Go to work, come home, cook for the kids. One night, she thought she would cook something different for a change. She had been watching the food channel and decided to prepare one of the recipes she saw on T.V. It turned out to be more work than she expected. She stood over the stove stirring the pot for what seemed to be an eternity. The kitchen was hot and she began to sweat until her hair turned limp.

She complained "Why don't they invent a self-stirring pot?"

Her son said, "That's a good idea. You could have a spoon that you could attach to the pot. You could have an electric motor that moves the spoon in a circle as the food cooks. "

Maggie's son was mechanical and liked tinkering with things. Together they created what they called THE WORLD'S FIRST SELF-STIRRING POT.

Maggie was excited about the invention and told her brother she was going to patent the invention. He tried to discourage her. "Patents cost a lot of money. Even if you saved enough for the patent and actually got one, what good would it be unless you could manufacture the pot and sell it?"

Maggie said "I could go to a company that makes pots and they could manufacture my pot."

Her sister-in-law also tried to talk her out of it. "Who would want such a pot? Stirring a pot is all part of cooking. If you enjoy cooking, you enjoy using a spoon to stir the food in a pot and then using the spoon to taste whether what you are cooking is properly seasoned. If you don't enjoy cooking, there's take-out, frozen food and the microwave oven. None of these need a pot."

Maggie disagreed. "There are people who like to cook but who don't want to spend time stirring a pot. And what about a handicapped person, or maybe someone who broke her arm?"

Her brother said, "Even if you could get a company to manufacture a pot and even if it was successful, it would only be a matter of time before another company puts out their own self-stirring pot and at a price lower than yours!"

Maggie answered, "But that's what patents are for. I could stop them from stealing my idea."

"That's just the point. You can't patent an idea, just the pot. Your pot has a spoon that goes clockwise, someone could design a spoon that goes counter-clockwise, up, down, and through the middle as well."

Maggie wasn't interested in logic. She had a dream and she was not about to give up on it. She went to the telephone book and looked up ATTORNEYS, PATENT.

The attorney listened carefully to Maggie. He told her just what she wanted to hear.

"That's a good idea. And I think we can get it patented. Do you know if anything like this is on the market?"

"No, I've never seen anything like it. It is strictly my own idea."

"The very first step in the patent process is for you to sign an Affidavit of Authenticity stating that there are no other self-stirring pots on the market."

"I never saw any for sale."

"That isn't good enough. I will need to conduct an investigation to be sure that is the case."

"What if you find one?"

"In that case, we need to see how your invention differs from the one on the market, and whether they are sufficiently different for you to get your own patent."

Maggie signed a retainer agreement for $200 an hour plus costs. She gave the attorney $5,000 to begin the process. A few months later the lawyer's legal assistant called with the good news. There was no other self-stirring pot on the market. She made an appointment for Maggie to come in to work with the lawyer to prepare to file the patent. At the meeting, the lawyer said he needed another $5,000 for the next step in the process.

He explained "Once I file the patent it will be assigned to a Patent Examiner who is knowledge-able in the field of cookware. The Examiner will want to see how your pot differs from all of the other pots that have been patented. You have taken an ordinary electrical motor to power the movement of the spoon. The motor will not be included in the patent unless you make some significant change to the motor. It is my job to negotiate with the Patent Office to get as much of your pot patented as possible."

It was a struggle, but Maggie scraped up another $5,000 and gave it to the lawyer.

The lawyer called her a few times within the next several months with progress reports. He continued to be optimistic about getting her the patent.

He explained how he had been negotiating with the Examiner to get the patent approved. But one day, he called with some bad news. The patent had been denied.

"It is not uncommon for the patent to be turned down on the first go-round. The Examiner has raised some issues that I feel confident that I can solve. I will need to redraft the application, but I will need another five thousand dollars to continue, not only to redraft the application but to negotiate with the Examiner as to what the final patent will cover ."

Maggie felt she was close to getting her patent so she sent another $5,000.

The lawyer called six months later with more bad news. His negotiations with the patent Examiner were dead-locked.

"The law allows an applicant, or his lawyer, to meet with the Examiner for exactly 60 minutes to explain, in person, the merits of the patent."

"But isn't the Patent Office in Washington, D.C.?"

"Yes, but I need to make the trip if we are going to ever get the patent. I will need another $5,000 to continue to pursue this."

Maggie was upset. "I can't keep giving you money with no end in sight."

"If I am successful, you should have your patent within the next few months."

"And this $5,000 will get me my patent?"

"I can't promise you that. If you are refused a second time, you can appeal the Patent Examiner's decision, but generally, it's two strikes and you're out. In your case, I believe we are very close to acceptance. You really do have a good invention."

Maggie felt trapped. She had already invested $20,000. If she didn't give him another $5,000 to go to Washington, it would be a complete loss.

"I only have $2,000 right now. Do you take credit cards?"

"Sure, just come into my office and my secretary will have you sign for it."

When the lawyer returned from Washington, he was up-beat. "The Examiner and I had a good meeting. There are still a few things we need to work out. But we are close."

Maggie finally did get her patent but the lawyer explained "This patent only covers the rotating rim of the pot. As I explained before, the motor is not included because you did not invent it. The pot and the spoon are not included because they are just like any other pot and spoon on the market. "

Her patent was less than she expected, but that did not upset Maggie as much as her lawyer telling her she would need to send almost $1,000 to the Patent Office for filing and publication fees. He said that in three and a half years she would need to send them another $500 to maintain the patent. In seven and a half years she would need to send them another $1,000 and in eleven and half years another $1,600.

"This is the fee charged by the federal government to protect your patent. Those fees are regularly changed by the government, so that subsequent maintenance fees might be higher. The $1,000 is the basic fee to protect it in the U.S. marketplace. But I recommend that you also pay a maintenance fee for the European market. Else they could market your pot and your patent would not be protected."

"Well, I guess this is not so much to pay to be sure that no one can copy my pot."

"Getting a patent doesn't guarantee that someone won't try to manufacture your pot without your permission. But if he does, you can tell him that you have a patent. You can demand that he either stop manufacturing your pot, or pay you for the right to use your invention. If he refuses you can sue him. He then has the right to defend against your law suit by challenging your patent in court. If you win the court battle, you can rest assured that your patent has been tested and is found to be valid."

It would be nice to say that Maggie sold her invention to a manufacturer and that she made a bundle. But she didn't. The self-stirring pot became just another dream that Maggie had to give up.

How To Defend Yourself Against
Your Patent Lawyer

Maggie made two basic mistakes. She made no effort to determine whether she had a marketable product before seeking a patent and she signed an open-ended retainer agreement without getting the whole picture. She needed to know a lot more about the field of cookware and the patent process before she embarked upon the venture. Her lawyer did not volunteer any information about the patent process and she did not know what questions to ask.

If you want to patent an invention, you need to find a patent attorney who will be up front with you and who will discuss its patentability.

PATENTABILITY

How much of your invention is patentable? Will you walk away with a marketable patent or will the patent be so narrow as to be worthless? Your lawyer will probably say he has no way of knowing the full extent of coverage until it gets to the Patent Examiner; however, he should be experienced enough in the field of your invention to give you his opinion about what the patent will cover.

EXPERIENCE

You will want an attorney who is a Registered Patent Attorney; meaning that he passed the Patent Bar examination and is now a member of the Patent Bar. You should see his Patent Bar membership certificate on his office wall next to his state license.

In addition to being a Registered Patent Attorney, you will want a patent attorney who is knowledgeable in the field of your invention. There are patent attorneys who do nothing but obtain patents related to computers. Others specialize in the field of bio-technology. It is important to employ someone who has worked with similar inventions in the past. He will have a better idea of the patentability of your invention than someone without any experience in the field. You need to ask the lawyer whether he considers himself to be an authority in the area of your patent, and if not, whether he knows of any attorney who is.

MARKETABILITY

Many law firms offer an invention evaluation as part of the initial consultation fee. They will give you an opinion as to whether your invention is patentable. Some firms go a step further and give you an opinion as to its marketability. They may even offer to help with the marketing of your invention. You need to have a clear understanding of what services your lawyer will provide for you.

THE RETAINER AGREEMENT

Do not expect the retainer agreement to say that your lawyer will obtain a patent for you. All that will be promised is that your lawyer will use his best efforts to get you a patent. Do expect your agreement to spell out costs you are responsible to pay.

Have your lawyer explain the steps in the process and the estimated cost of each step. Few lawyers will offer a fixed price contract to obtain a patent, but you may be able to negotiate an upper limit for each step. See Chapter 4 for an explanation of the Staged Fee Agreement.

Ask your lawyer how many of his patent applications have been accepted on the first go-round. This will give you some idea of whether he expects your patent to be rejected initially.

UNBUNDLING

There is a growing number of attorneys who offer guidance to their clients rather than full service representation. It is a mix between doing it yourself and having your attorney do it all. The attorney acts as a coach in certain areas of the case. In other areas, he takes over and does the legal work. This type of legal representation is called *unbundling*. The entire representation is considered to be a bundle of services for the client. Instead of offering a full bundle of services, the lawyer "unbundles" his services and assists the client in his own representation.

The Real Estate lawyer described in the second chapter of this book offered unbundled services to the seller of the home. He suggested she attend the closing without him, but promised to make himself available by telephone if some problem came up.

Not all patent attorneys are willing to unbundle their services. But for those who will, unbundling provides an opportunity to obtain a patent at a reasonable price. Those who offer unbundled services may encourage the client to conduct his own investigation to determine whether the invention has already been patented. The attorney will explain what steps are necessary to conduct a thorough investigation, and then review the investigation to be sure it is conducted properly.

How much the client participates after that depends on the complexity of the patent and the skill of the client. With unbundling representation, client and attorney need to have a clear understanding as to who is going to do what. It is important that they discuss the entire patent process at the beginning and then come to an agreement as to what service each will contribute.

OTHER OPTIONS

U.S. patents are good for up to 20 years from the filing date of the patent application. The length of the protection depends on the type of patent obtained. After the patent expires, the invention becomes part of the public domain and anyone can reproduce it.

Have your lawyer explain whether there are options available, other than a patent, that will protect your invention. For example, if you are a manufacturer and you have a process, tool or formula that is known only to you and your employees, then that is known as a *Trade Secret*. United States law protects Trade Secrets from being copied.

There is no time limit on Trade Secrets. They are forever. You may be better off keeping your invention as a Trade Secret rather than patenting it and losing your exclusive rights after a given number of years.

THE DIY PATENT

The story of Maggie is an example of someone who might have been better off trying to obtain her own patent. Her invention was a dream and not part of a realistic business plan. Even after she got the patent, she made no attempt to market her self-stirring pot. But her main problem was that she didn't do her homework. She had no concept of what was involved in the patent process, and Mr. Wrong Patent Lawyer wasn't about to tell her. Had he done so, she might have decided not to go forward in the first place.

Years ago, people had to rely on their lawyer to explain what is involved in getting a patent. In this, the information age, that is no longer the case. There are many web sites that explain the patent process. All you need to do is type PATENT into your favorite search engine for an overview of the subject.

Getting a patent is something many people do without any assistance from a lawyer. An explanation of the patent process and the forms that must be completed can be downloaded from the U.S. Patent and Trademark Office web site.
http://www.uspto.gov.

The Patent Office encourages inventors to seek their own patent. They offer monthly on-line question and answer sessions. During these sessions, senior officers of the Patent Office answer E-mail questions and offer tips to independent inventors.

Those with limited finances, who have a good idea, but no immediate marketing plan, might consider protecting that idea by obtaining a patent on their own. Of course, the idea itself is not patentable. It must be translated into something that can be patented.

If you have a good idea, you would do well not to share it with anyone until you file your patent. Under U.S. law you may lose your right to a patent if your idea is given public exposure more than a year prior to the filing. In many foreign countries, any public exposure prior to filing may cause the loss of patent rights. In this global economy, it is best to closely guard your idea until you file for the patent.

If you have something that you believe is going to be a money maker, and you have a business plan to market it, then this is not the time to DIY. You will want to take your idea to a Registered Patent attorney. He will document the date that you disclosed the idea to him. He should be able to tell you what type patent is best for you. There are few original ideas. Most inventions are the next step up from something that is currently on the market. If you have an idea to improve the appearance of something, he may recommend a *design patent*. If your idea relates to the working part of something currently on the market, he might suggest a *utility patent*.

Your lawyer should be willing to take the time to explain different options available to you and why he is recommending the suggested course of action.

Although our Mr. Wrong got Maggie a narrow patent (just the rim), your Mr. Right should be more successful at getting you a patent that covers more of your invention than you may have been able to obtain had you tried to get your own patent. Another important function is to help protect your patent once you market it. If anyone attempts to make, sell or use your invention without your permission, he can flex his legal muscles by calling or writing to them and demanding that they discontinue infringing on your patent. Should they ignore the warning, you can take the matter to court.

This is when you need your Patent Attorney most. He got that patent for you. He should be able to help defend the patent. That does not mean he will defend your patent without being paid to do so. Patent litigation is still litigation. Many Patent Attorneys restrict their practice to just obtaining the patent. They leave law suits to the trial lawyers. But your Patent Attorney should be able to refer you to a trial lawyer who is experienced in patent litigation. And your lawyer should be ready and willing to testify on your behalf should the matter go to trial.

Before you employ a Patent Attorney, you need to explore all of these avenues with him. Will he be available to call or write letters should someone infringe on your patent? How much will he charge to do so? Does he do patent litigation? If not, will he be available to testify on your behalf? How much will he charge to do so?

Getting this information up front will give you some idea of the cost should you need to defend your patent in court.

Some readers may think it a waste of time to worry about all this before you even apply for your patent. But the probability that you will need to defend your patent is directly proportional to the success of your invention. The more successful you are at marketing your invention, the greater the probability that someone will want to copy it.

STARTING A BUSINESS 14

He had one of those smiles you want to erase.

Susan didn't know why she hired this lawyer in the first place. Her gut told her he was not a nice guy when she met him. That he was not a successful lawyer was evident from the modest furnishings in his office and answering machine in place of a receptionist.

Susan asked what kind of law he practiced.

"Door law."

"What's that?"

"I practice anything that walks through the door," he laughed.

Susan dismissed this as one of those lawyer jokes. But she should have figured that he was a jerk and walked out. Instead she found herself explaining to him that she wanted to open her own crafts retail shop. She was well known in the art community as a talented artist. She created works in different mediums: wood, glass, fabric, ceramics. She sold her art works to retail stores, but her main source of income was from setting up booths at outdoor art shows throughout the country.

"I am tired of traveling. I want to have my own store here in town where I can sell my art works along with art supplies. I might give art lessons as well."

"Oh then, you'll want to form a corporation. That's the best protection for you. A person can sue the company, but not you personally."

Susan never thought of being sued with a crafts business, but she thought the lawyer knew what was best for her. She gave him $500 to form the corporation. She paid another $100 to cover the cost of filing the documents with the state. He did not ask her to sign a retainer agreement. She assumed the $600 would cover the complete job. She was surprised when he wanted another $500 when she went to his office to pick up the corporation kit that he ordered for her.

The kit was one of those form kits with the name of her company ARTZY & CRAFTY stamped in gold letters. The name was also stamped on her corporate seal. In addition, the kit contained stock certificates and the company minutes book. There were lots of forms in the minutes book. There was a page titled ORGANIZATIONAL MEETING. There were several pages of By-laws that spoke of pre-emptive rights, dissolution, and other legal things. She had no idea what any of this meant. She asked the lawyer what she was supposed to do with the kit, but he said he was late for court and had to leave. He said she could call him if she had any question.

How could she ask him a question? She didn't know enough to know what to ask. She decided to put the kit in her desk drawer and go about trying to lease a store front for her business.

She found a great location on Main Street. It was a small shop surrounded by other small businesses where mall-weary people liked to shop. The rent was high, but she thought she should be able to cover it with the income from her business.

The landlord gave her a lease to sign. Remembering that the lawyer said that no one could sue her personally if she did business as a corporation, she told him that the lease was to be in the company name. The landlord had no problem with that, but he added a paragraph at the bottom of the lease saying that Susan was personally responsible to pay the rent for the term of the lease, namely for the next five years.

He refused to lease the property to her unless she signed as guarantor. "You just formed this corporation. It could be out of business within six months. Then where would I be?"

Susan couldn't imagine that happening, so she agreed to guarantee the lease payments.

The lease also required her to obtain an insurance policy for one million dollars. She wondered why that was necessary.

The landlord explained, "Someone could come in and slip and fall. They could sue you and me. Insurance protects us both. You should take out a comprehensive policy. Your lease makes you responsible to pay for the storefront glass. It could be damaged in a storm, or maybe broken by a thief or a vandal. Because you are personally liable on the lease, you would be responsible to pay to repair it. Insurance is the best way to protect against these problems."

Susan was beginning to wonder why she formed a corporation in the first place. But those thoughts were forgotten in her excitement of getting the store ready for business. Within a few weeks the store was open and her first customer walked in. At least she thought he was a customer. He turned out to be the city inspector. "Where's your occupational license?"

"What's that?"

"You need to get a license from city hall before doing business in this town."

"This is my first business. I didn't know I needed a license."

"I could fine you for opening up without a license, but I'll give you a few days to get it."

Susan closed the shop early and went straight to city hall.

The clerk asked, "Where's your county occupational license? We can't issue the city license without it." The clerk told her where to get the county license. It was in an office almost 20 miles away. Susan rushed to get there before 5 p.m.

Susan was annoyed. She went to a lawyer to help her form a business. He charged her $1,100. For what? A kit with gold letters and a seal? But her annoyance turned to anger when it was time to pay her income taxes.

As with most small businesses, she lost money that first year. Her accountant asked "Why didn't you form an "S" corporation? You could have deducted your losses on your personal income tax and saved quite a bit in taxes."

"Shouldn't my lawyer have formed an "S" corporation for me ?"

"No. The corporation is formed with the state. The "S" corporation is formed by applying to the IRS. You needed to elect to make your company an "S" corp after the company was formed. But your lawyer should have told you about it. Actually, I don't know why you formed a corporation. You would have done better as a sole proprietor."

By now the reader knows all the things Susan should have done, starting with walking out of the door as soon as her instincts told her that this lawyer was Mr. Wrong.

How To Defend Against Your Lawyer
When Starting A Small Business

The first line of defense when seeking legal representation to form a business is to do your homework. You should have some idea of the different types of business organizations available so that you can explore your options with your lawyer.

Some readers may think this an unrealistic approach "How am I supposed to get this information? Isn't that what I am going to my lawyer to find out?"

Getting information about starting a small business is easy to do. The United States is the small business capital of the world. Chances are that you have a friend or relative who started a business at one time or another. Ask them to share their experiences with you.

You can get information from the Internet. Most state web sites contain a wealth of information about starting a business.

You can visit your local Chamber of Commerce. Most Chambers of Commerce have a Small Business mentor program. They may offer printed material about starting a business. Many Chambers hold seminars with local lawyers, accountants and financial planners available to answer questions.

Through these contacts, you should be able to find Mr. Right Business Lawyer.

EXPERIENCE

There are attorneys who specialize in business law, but generally their practice is limited to large companies with complex problems. Their fees are commensurate with their advanced legal skills (lawyer talk for "they are expensive").

You do not need this degree of specialization when you are starting out. An attorney with a general practice should be able to help you in setting up your own business. Should you have a special problem requiring the need for a business lawyer, he can refer one to you.

HONESTY

There are those readers who may want to give Susan's lawyer the benefit of the doubt. Maybe he wasn't being dishonest. Maybe he really believed that a corporation was the best protection for her.

But what he didn't tell her was the biggest lie of all.

He didn't tell her that it would cost her another $500 before he would give her the corporate kit.

He didn't tell her that most creditors will refuse to do business with her corporation unless she agreed to be personally responsible to pay company debts.

And what he probably knew, but didn't say, was that most businesses fail within the first three years, and that it may be better to postpone forming a corporation until you know you have a viable business.

To protect against this type of dishonesty, you need to require your lawyer to spend time with you to explore the different types of business organizations. If you are going to be the sole owner of the business, you need to ask him to compare the benefits of doing business as a sole proprietorship vs. a corporation.

If you are starting a partnership, you need to have him discuss the difference between a general partnership and a partnership with limited liability, such as a Limited Partnership. Like the sole proprietorship, each partner in a general partnership has full responsibility to pay the company debts. In a Limited Partnership only the managing partner is personally liable.

You need to compare these forms of partnership ownership with that of a corporation. It may be simpler in the long run to form a corporation and distribute the shares among the owners of the company. Whichever way you go, it is important to have a Partnership or Shareholder Agreement that defines each person's rights and responsibilities.

Going into business with someone is risky. A business partnership is much like a marriage. People enter the relationship with great hopes and expectations only to find they are terribly mismatched. The break-up of a partnership can be nastier than a divorce. Like a divorce, disagreements can be avoided if the parties have a written agreement saying how one party can buy out the share of the business owned by the other should things not work out.

If you decide to form a corporation with two or more people as owners of the company stock, you need a Shareholder's Agreement that serves the same function as a Partnership Agreement. The most important part of the Partnership or Shareholder's Agreement is how the shares of the company are to be evaluated in the event one of the parties wants to transfer his interest in the company, or in the event he dies.

There are any number of ways to evaluate a share of the business. The price of the share can be based on the annual income of the company, or it can be based on the appraised value of the assets of the company. It is important that your business attorney explain the different options that are available, and let you decide which method is best for you.

LOYALTY

When drafting a Shareholder or Partnership Agreement, it is important that your lawyer be concerned with your best interest and not that of your future partner. The reader may think that a strange requirement. Shouldn't the drafting attorney prepare an agreement that is fair to both parties? Yes, but the question is "What's fair?" Most people do not enter into a partnership equally. One person may be putting up most of the money while the other may be contributing the labor and expertise.

The lawyer who represents the monied partner needs to be concerned about protecting his client's investment. The lawyer who represents the partner who is going to contribute expertise or effort, needs to see to it that his client doesn't work for years, only to walk away with nothing.

The point is that one lawyer cannot be loyal to both parties. It's a conflict of interests. It is much like the lawyer who is drafting a pre-nuptial agreement. Under most state laws, he may not represent both the future husband and the future wife because they have opposing interests. If a couple visit a lawyer asking him to draft a pre-nuptial agreement for both of them, the ethical lawyer will refuse to do so until one of them employs his own lawyer.

Unfortunately, state laws offer no such protection for two people who go to a lawyer asking him to draft a partnership agreement. The lawyer may be ethically bound to ask one of them to seek his own representation, but this author knows of no state law requiring the lawyer to refuse to draft a partnership agreement on behalf of both parties.

Too often the future partners are concerned with the cost of employing a second lawyer and may insist on having the lawyer draft the agreement for both of them. Some lawyers may offer to "solve" the problem by having the parties sign a document saying that they agree to this dual representation. But signing such a document protects the lawyer, and not either party.

Should one party decide to attack the agreement at a later time, the lawyer will say that the agreement was designed to protect both parties. He will argue that if one party felt he was not adequately protected, he should have employed his own lawyer and not agreed to dual representation.

Signing a partnership agreement without your own lawyer to represent you may have serious financial consequences down the road. This is not the time to economize on attorney fees. You need someone to be squarely in your corner. You need someone to protect your interests; and your partner needs someone to protect his.

STARTING YOUR OWN BUSINESS

You don't need a lawyer to go into business as a sole proprietorship. There are many agencies on the state and local level that have programs designed to assist you. If you wish to start the business as a corporation, rather than as a sole proprietor, there are any number of legal kits on the market that you can use to form the corporation. As explained, you will need a lawyer if you decide to form a business partnership, or if you want to transfer shares of your corporation to someone.

Buying a business is not the time to DIY. You need a lawyer to be sure that the seller has full authority to sell the assets of the business, and that monies are not owed on the equipment. You also should check with your accountant to learn of the tax consequences of the purchase.

Buying into a franchise is another reason to seek legal counsel. The franchise documents the company puts before you have been prepared by the company lawyer for the benefit of the company. In most cases, they will not allow you to make changes to the prepared documents, but at least your lawyer will be able to explain the legal effect of signing the documents. Having your lawyer explain what you are getting into may make you more comfortable with the deal, or you may decide that this is not the kind of commitment you want to make. Either way, an appointment with Mr. Right Business Lawyer should be well worth the consultation fee.

BANKRUPTCY   15
THE AMERICAN WAY OF DOING BUSINESS

That first year in business was hard for Susan. She struggled to make the monthly rental, not only on her business lease but on her apartment as well. The only bright spot that year was meeting Arturo. He was an up and coming artist who was here from Venezuela to show his works at an art gallery. She met him at the gallery. She was surprised to learn how much they had in common. He was interested in expanding his works by using different mediums. He admired the work she did in glass, wood and ceramics. She was interested in painting in oils and that was his forte.

He admired her willingness to take risks by opening her own business. She confessed that she had more courage than brains. If she stopped to think about it she might not have started the venture, but now she was stuck with a five year lease. She complained that she was struggling to make a go of it.

He said he had just sold several of his paintings and would be happy to help her out financially. She was surprised at his offer, but shocked the following week when he asked her to marry him. "But we just met."

"Don't you believe in love at first sight?"

"Yes, but we hardly know each other."

Susan was flattered that an artist of his stature would be interested in her. That and his persistent, and insistent pursuit of her, convinced her to marry. He didn't want to take the time to plan a large wedding, so they had a small ceremony with a few of her friends and relatives present.

After the wedding, Arturo moved into Susan's apartment. She helped him unpack his belongings. She noticed a letter from a lawyer saying that he was processing Arturo's papers to have him become a citizen. The letter was dated the day after their wedding. When she asked him about it, he said "Don't you want us to be together always? I need to become a citizen if I am going to stay by your side. "

Arturo busied himself at the store. He set up a studio in the back so he could paint without being disturbed. True to his word he made all of her business payments current. He purchased additional inventory and set about redecorating the shop. One day he announced that the shop needed a new name. "Artzy & Crafty is too cutsy. We are going to call this ART'S CRAFTS."

Susan felt that he was being bossy and let him know about it. He ignored her, and painted his name on the storefront window. That was not their only disagreement. After his initial contribution, Arturo made no attempt to contribute to their support. All he did was paint. When Susan asked him to sell some of his works, he refused.

"I cannot sell a painting until I am finished with it. This series of paintings needs more work. I have a reputation to uphold. If I turn out a lesser work, it will damage my status as an artist."

"I don't see anything wrong with your paintings. They all look great to me. If you think one of them needs more work, get it done and let's sell it."

He said he would. But he didn't. Susan tried to support them from the store income; but the name change, new decor and additional inventory did little to increase sales. She soon found herself in worse shape than before. She fell behind in her lease payments. All of her credit cards were maxed out. The telephone company discontinued service. Actually, she was happy they did. Arturo ran up hundreds of dollars in calls to Venezuela on her telephone bill. In fact, all of the bills were in her name only. Nothing was in his name. It was only Susan's credit that was being ruined.

Finally she decided to file for bankruptcy. Arturo was all for it, "That's the American Way of doing business. Declare bankruptcy and wipe out all your debts. Then you can close the store and start fresh. Maybe get a job."

This time Susan was careful in choosing a lawyer. She found an attorney who specialized in bank-ruptcy. She did not get a chance to speak to him when she called, however the receptionist made an appointment for her to meet with him the next day.

The lawyer's office was nicely furnished but not elaborate. It was a busy place. She could see two legal assistants in one office, a lawyer working in the law library and another in his office speaking on the telephone. The receptionist took her into the conference room where she waited for the lawyer. A nice looking young man came in.

"Are you the lawyer?"

"No, I'm his legal assistant. He's on a conference call. He asked me to get some preliminary information so we can save time."

The legal assistant had a form sheet which he completed. He explained the bankruptcy procedure to Susan and told her she would qualify for a Chapter 7 bankruptcy filing.

"What's that?"

"You should be able to have all debts forgiven. You should be able to keep your car and your personal belongings, but you will need to liquidate your store inventory to repay as much of your debts as you are able."

"How long will this take?"

"You will need to go before the Trustee to verify that you are eligible for Chapter 7."

"What's a Trustee?"

"He's a court appointed official. Something like a judge. Once he verifies that everything you said in your bankruptcy filing is true, you will receive your discharge order releasing you from your debts. It usually takes two or three months after the hearing to get your order. "

"What will the Trustee ask of me?"

"Oh, you don't need to worry about that. Your lawyer will be with you. He knows what information the Trustee will want and he will have it ready for the hearing."

At that point the attorney walked in. The legal assistant gave him the form he had completed. The lawyer agreed that Susan should qualify for a Chapter 7 bankruptcy filing. He said his fee was $1,500 to do the bankruptcy. He gave her a retainer agreement that said he would not be responsible to file the bankruptcy until he was paid in full.

"I thought I told you that I'm broke. Where am I supposed to get that money?"

"Some people borrow money from friends or family. You could have a half price sale and sell off your inventory. One way or another you will need to sell it. I see you've been paying $500 a month on your credit card debt. You can give me part of that payment. You should be able to pay me in a couple of months and then I will file for Chapter 7."

Susan sent as much money to her lawyer as she was able during the next few months. Once she mailed her final payment, she called and made an appointment with her lawyer.

At the meeting she was greeted by a different legal assistant. "Your lawyer had an emergency court hearing and he asked me to begin to prepare for the Chapter 7 filing."

It was obvious to Susan that this legal assistant was most experienced in preparing cases for bankruptcy, so she was not concerned that her attorney couldn't be present for her appointment. She was concerned when her lawyer did not appear at the hearing. In his place was still another new face. "Where's my lawyer?

"He wasn't able to make it today, but he and I work closely together and I know all about your case."

"Are you a lawyer?"

"Oh yes, our law firm has several lawyers. All experienced in bankruptcy law."

They went into the hearing together. Susan was surprised that it took a only few minutes. The Trustee asked a few questions. Her lawyer had all of her paper work in order. When they left he said the hearing had gone very well and she should have the trustee's order discharging her debts within a few months. And so she did.

You may think that Susan finally did something right. She choose an attorney who did nothing but bankruptcies and she got her order of discharge relatively quickly. But her lawyer was deficient in two areas: Honesty and Conscientiousness.

HONESTY

Although Susan thought $1,500 a lot of money, it wasn't much to pay for the work that was necessary in order to get an order of discharge. But fees charged by lawyers for bankruptcy are hemmed in by the ability of the client to pay and by the bankruptcy laws.

The one thing people who file for bankruptcy don't have is an abundance of cash. There's just so much the client can pay to the lawyer, so he is limited in the amount he can charge. The second limiting factor is that bankruptcy laws require the lawyer to charge a "reasonable" fee. The Trustee will ask how much the lawyer is charging the client. If that fee is significantly above the going rate in that particular area of the country, it will be challenged by the Trustee as not being reasonable.

Lawyers who limit their practice to bankruptcy need to operate most efficiently in order to generate a good income. That means employing legal assistants to do much of the work. It was dishonest of Susan's lawyer to lead her to believe that he would be doing the work.

He should have had the courtesy to greet her when she came in for her first meeting. He should have explained to her she would be working with his legal assistant, but that he would be with her at the appearance before the Trustee. And then he should have been there himself instead of sending another lawyer in his place.

Most people understand the lawyer's need to have the assistance of a legal assistant. It helps keep down the cost of legal services while enabling a lawyer to carry a heavier case load. If a client objected to working with a legal assistant, he would be free to seek other legal counsel. By not telling Susan how he intended to operate, her lawyer denied her the opportunity to make her own decision about whether she wanted to work with a non-lawyer to prepare her bankruptcy case.

CONSCIENTIOUSNESS

Susan's lawyer is the classic example of someone who is over extended. The only time she saw him is when he gave her a retainer agreement. He did not take the time to really look at her problem to determine whether there were other avenues to follow other than a Chapter 7 bankruptcy. Her financial problems originated with her business. He could have discussed a business reorganization as allowed under Chapter 11 of the bankruptcy law. A Chapter 11 might have allowed her to stay in business while reorganizing her debts to pay some or all of her creditors.

He might have explored methods of solving her financial problems without the need to file for bankruptcy. There are for-profit and not-for-profit organizations who assist people by negotiating with creditors to reduce monthly payments, or to forgive some portion of the debt for immediate payment.

He did none of these things. He relied on his legal assistant's assessment of Susan's finances and with a typical "lawyer knows best" attitude, advised a Chapter 7 bankruptcy proceeding to wipe out all her debts — and her business along with it.

It may have been that Susan would have come to the same conclusion had she been presented with all of this information. But the point is, she should have been given the opportunity to make that decision herself.

Finally, the lawyer should have discussed debt management with Susan at some point in his representation. Susan was a lady much in need of financial guidance. She got none of that from her lawyer.

How much easier would it have been if Susan had a lawyer who had taken the time to offer suggestions about ways she could manage her finances and rebuild her credit?

How To Defend Against
Your Bankruptcy Attorney

By now you know the best way to protect against your bankruptcy lawyer is to have some idea of what bankruptcy is about before you call for an appointment. That information is easy to come by. Go to your favorite Internet search engine and type in the word bankruptcy. If you don't have a computer, ask your friends or relatives to help by printing out bankruptcy information on their computer.

By learning about the bankruptcy procedure and basic terminology associated with the process, you will know what questions to ask your attorney. You will want him to explain which Chapter in bankruptcy he recommends and why he thinks it is best for you. You will want to explore whether a bankruptcy is necessary, or whether a reputable credit counseling company can help you work through your creditor problems.

Once you know what questions to ask, the next line of defense is to look for Mr. Right Bankruptcy Lawyer. The example given in this chapter was that of a bankruptcy mill. They work on volume. They are usually efficient and effective. They get the job done and in most cases for a reasonable price. If you have done your homework and you know exactly which Chapter is right for you, you well might seek a firm who does nothing but bankruptcies.

But if you are not sure about the best way to go, you may want to seek an attorney who regularly does bankruptcy as part of his general or business practice. You will want to find someone who will take the time to explore all of your options and then help you to choose the best path.

It may be that with his assistance you will not need to file for bankruptcy. It may cost you less to work through your financial problems than if you had filed for bankruptcy.

The thing that is often lacking in a bankruptcy mill is personal attention. If you are going through a financial crisis, maybe what you need more than help in filing for bankruptcy is someone who will guide you past this difficult time in your life.

THE DIY BANKRUPTCY

The American Bankruptcy Institute web site contains a table that gives the number of households per bankruptcy filing. For the year 2003, they reported a national average of 73.1. This means that for every 73 households in the United States, one of them filed for bankruptcy in 2003. The American Bankruptcy Institute also publishes a chart that compares the number of bankruptcy filings to the consumer debt payments as a percentage of disposable personal income. You might think that the greater the debt, the greater number of bankruptcies filed. But the chart shows no such correlation. The number of bankruptcies filed has been steadily increasing while the debt has remained relatively stable. In 1986 the debt was 14%. There was less than 500,000 bankruptcies filed that year. In 2002, once again the debt was 14%, only this time over 1,500,000 people filed for bankruptcy.

There are other forces at work other than percent of debt that are causing this increase in bankruptcy filings. Bankruptcy attorneys are reporting an increase in bankruptcy filings by the elderly. The problem is the high medical cost of maintaining those who are aged. Those with a fixed income are struggling to cover the rising cost of their medical care. They may run up medical bills that they are unable to pay. In many states, a person's home is a protected asset, so creditors cannot force the sale of the property, but once the person dies, their creditors can require the home to be sold to pay those bills.

Children of the debtor may be concerned that instead of inheriting a house, all they will be left with is a mountain of debt. Increasingly the children are encouraging their parents to get rid of the debt by filing for bankruptcy.

All this has not gone unnoticed by congress. Bankruptcy laws were not designed to protect an inheritance, nor were the laws designed to encourage people to live beyond their means. With considerable nudging from the credit card industry, Congress is discussing revisions to the bankruptcy laws that will make it more difficult to obtain bankruptcy protection.

In the event that Congress changes the law, it will be important for those who want to file for bankruptcy to consult with an attorney who can explain the changes in the law. Those who wish to file for bankruptcy under the present law can do so on their own, provided they are willing to put in the time and effort to learn about the bankruptcy procedure.

If you decide to DIY, you still will be well served to have at least one consultation with a bankruptcy attorney. He can suggest which plan is best for you. Also, there are variations in the bankruptcy laws, state to state. He will be able to explain how the laws of your state will impact your bankruptcy filing.

Greeting The Immigrant 16
with open pocketbooks

Arturo couldn't remember when he first decided to go to America and become a citizen. To him, it was the only place to be. He made a special effort to learn English at school. He prided himself in being able to converse fluently in the language. His other passion in life was his art.

His family didn't understand this obsession with the states. They didn't understand his art either.

His father asked, "What's your problem? Haven't I always provided for you? You have a family who loves you. Why do you want to go away? America can't be any more beautiful than Venezuela. What are you looking for that you don't already have here?"

Arturo couldn't answer because he didn't know what he was looking for. He just knew that he had to follow his dream, and the United States was part of that dream.

Over the years he worked hard at his art. He achieved some success as a painter. He was over-joyed when an art gallery invited him for a showing of his work in the states. Before he left he asked his lawyer to locate a good immigration lawyer and make an appointment for him.

Arturo went straight from the airport to the lawyers's office. "I want to be a U.S. citizen as quickly as possible."

"Well you can't ask for asylum because you certainly have not been treated badly at home. One way you can stay and apply for citizenship is if you happen to fall in love and marry."

The next day Arturo met Susan and as the saying goes "the rest is history" or in this case, as in the previous chapter.

Arturo met with his immigration lawyer on a regular basis over the next three years. The lawyer cautioned that the immigration authorities would be suspicious of his motives in marrying Susan. He said they would conduct an investigation to see whether they really were living together as husband and wife.

Arturo protested, "Of course she's my wife. We love each other. I wouldn't know what I would do without her. We have our own business together. I have nothing to hide. Let them investigate."

Arturo prepared Susan for the interview with the U.S. Citizen and Naturalization Services ("USCIS"), formerly known as the Immigration and Naturalization Service ("INS").

Susan was surprised that she was being investigated. She knew that Arturo was seeking citizenship. She didn't know that he based his application on their marriage. She began to suspect that he might have married her just to become a citizen. But she soon talked herself out of such dark thoughts. Arturo was handsome and talented. He could have had his pick of any number of attractive ladies. Why would he have married her unless he loved her?

The investigation of their marriage was lengthy and thorough. Finally the immigration authorities concluded that they were indeed living together as husband and wife. If it was a marriage for his convenience, it surely was not for hers. All he did was paint all day. She supported him, cooked for him, kept a clean house for him. Why would any woman do that except for love?

Arturo employed his lawyer on an hourly basis. The investigation added to his growing attorney bill. Luckily Arturo had his own savings account in Venezuela and was able to pay his lawyer the thousands of dollars it took to get his citizenship.

The day he was sworn in as a citizen was a happy day for Arturo, but he chose not to share it with Susan. He left her the next day, and then filed for divorce.

And yes, he took all of his valuable paintings with him.

You might think we have no words of criticism about Arturo's lawyer. He got the job done, but as with Susan's bankruptcy lawyer there was much to be desired.

How To Defend Against
Your Immigration Lawyer

HONESTY

You may have picked up on the fact that Arturo's lawyer was less than honest when he suggested that Arturo "fall in love" and marry. The reader may think that the lawyer was only trying to help his client. But the problem is the one raised in the first chapter of this book, namely integrity.

The lawyer was in effect encouraging his client to defraud the government. When he became a lawyer he took an oath to uphold the laws of the United States. If your lawyer can't be true to his sworn oath, why expect him to be honest with you?

But there is a practical reason not to employ a dishonest Immigration lawyer. It's reputation. The USCIS soon comes to know which immigration lawyers follow the law and which try to detour around it. They knew all about this lawyer's propensity to represent clients who were trying to become citizens based on marriage. They gave Arturo a much harder time than if he were represented by a reputable lawyer. Hard time equals high attorney fees.

A reputable attorney would have explained all of the other ways he could have become a citizen. If Arturo decided, on his own, to base his application on his marriage, it might have cost him far less than what he ultimately paid his dishonest lawyer.

THE RETAINER AGREEMENT

Cost is an important consideration. Most firms offer an open-ended hourly fee agreement. Do not expect the agreement to promise success, just that the lawyer will use his best efforts to achieve your goal. Your lawyer cannot promise that you will become a citizen because the USCIS investigation might reveal something that would stop you from remaining in the U.S. Those immigrants with a criminal record in their homeland, or who commit a crime while applying for citizenship, can expect to be deported.

Although he cannot promise the outcome you seek, an experienced lawyer knows what steps need to be taken. He has a good idea of how much time he will need to spend at each stage of representation. If you cannot negotiate a fixed price agreement, try to get him to agree to a Staged Fee Agreement as described in Chapter 4.

EXPERIENCE

You will want to employ an attorney who is experienced enough to have a track record with USCIS. And be sure he is an attorney. There are too many companies that use the words "Immigration" and "law services" in their advertisement that are not legal firms. These companies help people complete the USCIS forms, for a price, but they are no more than paper-filler-outers. So too are people who call themselves "Notarious." This is the Latin American name for a notary public. But in Latin America, a Notorious has more legal status than does a notary public here in the states.

Latin American immigrants see the name Notarious and think they are employing someone with the legal background of the Notarious of their homeland. However, here in the U.S., the Notarious has no more right to practice law than does a notary public. Yet they charge significant funds to help the immigrant complete relatively simple forms.

The worst case scenario is that they make a mistake in completing the application that puts the immigrant on the deportation list. If a lawyer made such a mistake, he could be held accountable. He could lose his license. The non-lawyer, being unlicensed, is not accountable.

CONSCIENTIOUSNESS

The bankruptcy mill described in the last chapter has its counterpart in the immigration mill. The law firm does nothing but immigration. They generally have a large staff of lawyers and legal assistants with the ability to accommodate clients who are unable to speak English.

Expect efficient and effective service from such a law firm. But, like the bankruptcy mill, the one thing that may be lacking is the personal interaction with someone who knows your case and who is "your" lawyer.

If you decide to employ a large immigration firm, you need someone to take the time to explain all of the avenues available to you, instead of allowing them to choose a course of action that you follow blindly. Listen to what is being recommended, and then ask, "Are there other ways to achieve my goal?"

Once you decide upon a path, you need to have a clear understanding of what the firm intends to do for you. The lawyer should be willing to take the time to outline each step in the process. You need to know who is going to do the actual work. You should ask whether you will be working with the lawyer, or whether he will just supervise the work of the legal assistant. Finally, you need to know what to expect in terms of the time it will take to complete your case.

If you are trying to become a U.S. citizen, it can take anywhere from 5 months to over two years before your interview with the USCIS. If all goes well with the interview, it can take up to six months before you attend the swearing in ceremony. If your application is not approved it could take a year or two to straighten out the problem — and depending on the problem, maybe never.

You need to be able to have someone in the firm with whom you can communicate on a regular basis. You will be spending significant sums of money. You should be assured that you will get good service for your money before you sign the retainer agreement.

Employing a small or medium size firm does not automatically assure prompt and individual attention. Look for signs that the lawyer is over-extended or under-staffed: telephone interruptions during your initial consultation; an untidy or disorganized office with files all over the place; a lawyer who looks distracted when you speak to him. If you can't get his attention at this first meeting, don't expect anything different down the line.

With Immigration Law, communication is the most important thing. Nothing will upset you more than not being told what is going on. Give your lawyer a plus if he says that he will give you a copy of everything he files. Give him a plus plus if he asks "Do you want me to call you with progress reports or should I send you an e-mail?"

THE DIY CITIZEN

The U.S. Immigration law is designed for people to do it themselves. Tens of thousands of immigrants have applied for and became citizens on their own. Yet tens of thousand have been refused citizenship and have been deported back to their homeland. The question the immigrant needs to ask is whether there is anything about his application that might trigger deportation. If so, he would be foolhardy to DIY.

The second most important reason to seek the counsel of an attorney is that there are so many options offered by the U.S. Citizenship and Immigration Services that you should consult with a lawyer at least once so he can explain what is available to you, given your set of circumstances.

For those with good English reading skills, there is a wealth of information on the USCIS web site, from the history of the Immigration Service to a description of all of the options available to a non-citizen, to application forms that can be down-loaded.
http://uscis.gov

If you decide to DIY it is important that your application be completed truthfully and accurately. If you make a mistake you can delay the process for years. If you lie on your application, you could be deported. Even if your secret is not discovered by USCIS, in this information age, it could be discovered after you become a citizen and you could still be deported.

Employing Mr. Right Immigration Lawyer protects you even after you become a citizen. That was the case with Manuel. A few months after becoming a citizen, he decided to go back to Mexico for a visit. He was stopped at the airport by the immigration authorities. They did a computer check of his name and then took his passport away. "You were arrested for possession of drugs before you came to the states. You must have obtained your citizenship illegally."

Manuel was allowed a telephone call which he placed to his Immigration lawyer. The lawyer came right down and chided the Immigration authorities. "Don't you have enough to do catching illegal aliens? Now you are bothering U.S. citizens? I processed Manuel's application. Here is a copy of that application. As you can see, he made a full and complete disclosure of that minor drug offense he committed as a teenager. The Immigration Service knew all about it. They had no problem with it and neither should you."

Manuel's passport was returned and he went on his way after profuse expressions of gratitude to his lawyer.

IT'S YOUR LEGAL SYSTEM 17
YOU CAN CHANGE IT

As the reader completes this book, he may be thinking that a better title for the book might have been HOW TO DEFEND AGAINST THE WHOLE LEGAL SYSTEM.

The examples given describe problems in the legal system from the U.S. Supreme Court down to notary publics who engage in the illegal, and unlicensed practice of Immigration Law.

The most important function of Mr. Right Lawyer is to uphold the law. But in many cases his efforts are hampered by the system itself. I call it legal corruption. What some people in the judicial system are doing is legal, but none-the-less, corrupt.

There's no point to hand wringing. Complaining about a corrupt system only encourages more corruption. Those who abuse their authority are encouraged by the knowledge that the general public is aware of what is going on, and does nothing to stop it. This is the same as condoning the corruption. And that was certainly not the intent of this author.

My reason to write the book was to expose corruption in our legal system, but more importantly, to encourage the reader to do something about it.

The first "do something" is to start a dialogue on the topic of legal corruption. Readers can share their experiences with each other and with me by going to the FORUM section of the Eagle Publishing Company Web site.

http://www.eaglepublishing.com

The second "do something" is to present ways the proactive reader can change the system.

It's Your System of Justice
FIX IT

STOP THE UNAUTHORIZED PRACTICE OF LAW

The self-help legal industry is a growth industry. There are all sorts of books, legal kits and web sites that offer information about how to DIY. Self representation is the right of every citizen. As discussed in this book, there are many times when self help is appropriate.

The problem arises when a person tries to prepare a legal document and is not too sure about how to do so. He may go to a company that advertises the services of a person who will assist in completing legal documents. Such businesses are not illegal. But giving legal advice while completing the form is. Too often the customer asks a question and the non-lawyer offers a legal explanation which may, or may not, be correct.

Unfortunately, people with little money, and little understanding of our legal system, are being targeted by these non-lawyers. Because of the language barrier, immigrants are most susceptible to such mis-representation. As explained in the last chapter, serious problems can arise when a non-lawyer gives bad legal advice. It can lead to deportation.

The person giving the advice can't lose his license because he doesn't have one. The immigrant has the right to complain to the authorities about being given bad legal advice, but because they do not have legal status, they hesitate to do so.

The problem of the unauthorized practice of law is not easily solved. The reader can do his part by refusing legal advice from a non-lawyer. Those who have immigrant family and friends should encourage them to seek counseling from a law firm and not a street vendor.

For those who cannot afford legal fees, there are Legal Service organizations that offer legal representation for little or no money, depending on the client's circumstances. You can find a list of Legal Services agencies that are available throughout the United State at the web site of the American Bar Association. http://www.abanet.org.

LEGISLATIVE ACTION

In most states, the unauthorized practice of law is a misdemeanor, with the penalty, a small fine. This is not likely to deter the person who has a growing unauthorized "practice." One way to put a damper on the growth of companies that engage in the unauthorized practice of law is to increase the penalty.

You can help by contacting your legislator. Each state elects delegates from local districts to their state legislature. You can ask the state representative from your county whether the unlicensed practice of law is punishable as a misdemeanor or as a felony. You can suggest to your representative that the penalty for the unlicensed practice of law be increased to the point that it will deter people from engaging in that practice.

Most state web sites contain the telephone number and e-mail address of state representatives. You can find a list of state web sites at the Public Information section of Eagle Publishing Company.

http://www.eaglepublishing.com

In Chapter 4, we described the actions of a corrupt court reporter who changed the record to protect the lawyer who hired her. This was not an imaginary case. It happens so frequently in the real world that lawyers have a name for such action. They call it "sanitizing" the record.

If you are in a state that licenses court reporters and you find that a court reporter has doctored the record in your case, you can lodge a complaint with the state licensing agency. With or without state licensing, you can protect the record of your case by requiring your attorney to employ a court reporter who is loyal to him and who does not regular work for the opposing law firm.

LEGISLATIVE ACTION

You can learn whether your state requires court reporters to be licensed by calling the NATIONAL COURT REPORTERS ASSOCIATION at (800) 272-6272 or visit their web site at http://www.NCRAonline.org. If your state does not require court reporters to be licensed, contact your state representative and ask him to start legislative action to pass a bill requiring such licensing. Also ask him to require that all court reporters use a recorder as part of their equipment. Modern court recording equipment utilizes a computer that records what is being said as the court reporter types in the testimony being given. Having such equipment will make it difficult to change the record.

In Chapter 3, we described the practice of the clerk of the court assigning cases to certain judges as a favor to the lawyer. We were being kind. Too often the assignment is given, not as a favor, but for money. Correcting this problem is not as easy as firing the clerk. There is someone who supervises the counter clerk, but that person is probably just as corrupt. It is hardly likely that the person in charge of the clerk is not aware of what is going on.

The average citizen is not concerned about these courthouse "politics." For one reason, many court systems are so small that there is only one judge for a given area of law. There is no choice because there is only one Probate judge, one criminal court judge, etc. The clerk gets to assign a judge only in county large enough to have several judges available for a given area of law. Correcting the problem in large counties is difficult because of public apathy. Most people never see the inside of a courthouse. Even if a person is are aware that clerks are playing favorites they may not want to get involved, "This is a lawyer problem. Let them solve it."

Easier said than done. Each courthouse is a small community of clerks, administrators, lawyers, bailiffs, judges and their legal assistants. They all work together. If one of the lawyers were to attack the system as being corrupt, he would be treated the same as any whistle-blower in our society. He could expect some very rough treatment from that legal community.

I never met a lawyer brave enough to take on the system. To do so he would need to accuse a clerk of favoritism, and to publicly criticize a judge as being a poor judge. No, lawyers take the easier route of trying to get in the good favor of the clerk so that next time he gets the good judge. Leave the bad judges for the new lawyers fresh out of law school, or the unsuspecting out of town lawyer who files a case in this court.

The reader should be concerned about the problem for three reasons. The first is philosophic. The court is the only place to go for those who seek justice. How can you expect justice if you allow corruption at this initial stage of the case? The second reason is pragmatic. The next case assigned may be yours. You should have a fair chance at having a good judge assigned to hear your case. The third reason is that the problem is easily fixed at the legislative level.

LEGISLATIVE ACTION

The solution to the problem is to take the assignment of cases out of the hands of the clerk. The technology is there to see that judges are assigned on a rotating basis. When someone files a case, a computer should automatically assign the next case number together with the judge who will preside over the case. Courthouses now have computer facilities. You can ask your representative to require that the computer be programed to assign a judge along with the case number.

Writing the series *Guiding Those Left Behind* gave me a bird's eye view of the Probate laws of different states. The thing that impressed me most was the great variation state to state in rights given to the beneficiaries of a Probate Estate. In Chapter 6, we discussed how little control a beneficiary has over the Probate procedure. But it doesn't need to be that way. In Kentucky, if the Personal Representative is the sole beneficiary of the Estate, he can close out the Estate after six months and transfer all of the property to himself by filing an affidavit with court verifying that all bills and taxes have been paid. Why don't other states allow the same?

In California, beneficiaries can use an affidavit to transfer up to $100,000 of the decedent's personal property without going through Probate. It works in California. It can work in any other state.

At the end of Chapter 7, we discussed the right of an attorney to be appointed as Personal Representative and to use Estate funds to pay himself as Personal Representative AND as attorney for himself. Most states allow this double-dipping. But it is a conflict of interest for a lawyer to pay himself to represent himself. In this author's opinion, this is legal corruption and should not be allowed.

In state after state, I found Probate laws that profit no one but the lawyers. It doesn't need to be that way.

But the problem with changing Probate laws is citizen apathy. Most of us will have no Probate experience during our lifetime. Why worry about something that doesn't concern us? Those who go through an unhappy Probate experience are not inclined to do anything to change the system. They don't expect to ever go through another Probate procedure, so why spend their time trying to change things?

And so the legal corruption continues.

LEGISLATIVE ACTION

Most people inherit relatively modest Estates. People who inherit personal property worth less than $100,000 should not be required to "share" their inheritance with a lawyer. Ask your legislator to investigate the small Estate procedure that is in effect in California and then explain to you why your state doesn't have a similar plan.

Ask your legislator whether the Probate laws of your state allow an attorney to pay himself as Personal Representative and also as the lawyer for the Personal Representative. And don't let your legislator wiggle out of the issue by saying that the lawyer isn't really representing himself, he is representing the Probate Estate. The lawyer is paying himself and no matter how he tries to justify that action, it is still a conflict of interest.

Each chapter of this book gave an example of Mr. Wrong Lawyer. Yet there was only one example of a client who called the Bar to complain (Ethel in Chapter 6). They did nothing to help her other than recommend that she employ still another lawyer to fix the problem.

In other chapters, we described the actions of Mr. Wrong, but the client made no complaint because they were not aware that their lawyer was doing anything wrong. That was the case with the bankruptcy client and the immigration client.

Those who know they have been wronged can call the state licensing agency. In most states, the state Bar is the licensing agency for attorneys. Attorneys must belong to the Bar and follow the laws regulating their conduct as an attorney. Most Bar Associations come down hard on any lawyer who is convicted of a serious crime or who uses his client's trust funds for his own personal gain.

But for most other matters, filing a Bar complaint is like pushing an elevator button several times. It might make you feel like you're doing something, but you are not. A survey conducted in Florida showed the few people who turn to the Bar for assistance receive any kind of satisfaction.

The Florida Bar formed a Special Commission on Lawyer Regulation. It examined the results of a survey on the Bar's Grievance Process. The survey was answered by *Complaintants* (those who filed the complaint), the *Respondents* (the lawyers against whom the complaint was filed), the Respondent's lawyers, the Referee who tried to have the parties resolve the complaint and the Grievance Committee who finally decided the case.

The results of that survey was published in June, 2004. Satisfaction with the appropriateness of the Grievance Case Decisions ranged from 14% to 97%. What group do you think was most dissatisfied with the results and what group most satisfied with the results? If you guessed the Complaintants were most dissatisfied and the Grievance Committee who made the decision were most satisfied, you already know the extent of the problem.

	% Satisfied with decision	% Dissatisfied with decision
Complaintants	14%	86%
Respondent's lawyer	72%	28%
Referee	83%	17%
Respondents	87%	13%
Grievance Comm.	97%	3%

This survey is typical of what is happening throughout the country; namely, few people who file a complaint with the Bar are satisfied with the results.

LEGISLATIVE ACTION

Most state Bars keep a record of reprimands and punishments. If they punish a lawyer with a fine, suspension, or removal of his license, that action becomes part of his record. If the Bar determines that the lawyer did nothing to warrant a reprimand or a punishment, the record of the complaint never appears in his file. If a client calls asking about the lawyer's record, he will be told that the lawyer has a clean record.

This is misleading to the public. The public should be able to find out how many complaints were filed against the lawyer and the result of the investigation. Some readers (lawyers, no doubt) will protest that this is like saying a lawyer is guilty until proven innocent. But I say that publishing such information will change the way lawyers treat their clients. As it now stands, only the most serious complaints are punishable by the Bar. Lawyers know that all they need to do is answer the complaint and present their side of the dispute to the Bar. The client receives no satisfaction unless the client can prove that the lawyer actually did something wrong.

If the lawyer knew that a complaint filed against him would remain part of his record, he might try not to let that happen. Protection for the lawyer could be built into the system such as requiring lawyer and client to attend mediation to try to work out the problem before the client is allowed to file a complaint.

If they can't work it out, the Bar will investigate the matter and make the results part of the lawyer's file.

You can ask your legislator to implement this plan, but expect resistance. In most states, the Bar is the regulatory agency. The Bar is composed of lawyers; so lawyers are regulating themselves. If the number of complaints and the resulting action taken by the Bar is published on the Internet, the public will not only be able to decide which lawyers are doing a good job, they will be able to decide whether the Bar is doing a good job of policing its own.

HOLD JUDGES ACCOUNTABLE

The law says you are entitled to a fair hearing, but increasingly, that is not the case. As explained in the divorce chapter, this has become such a problem that groups have been formed to monitor the court behavior of those judges with a poor reputation. Although such groups have no legal authority, they serve an important function by shinning a light on abuses within the judiciary.

But we need more than publicity. We need to take a serious look at the way judges are appointed. In some states, judges are elected to the bench. In other states, they are appointed by a government agency. The problem with government appointments is that they are political. Judges are not selected for their exemplary record or their exceptional legal skills. They are elected because of their party affiliation. And that is an invitation for abuse.

LEGISLATIVE ACTION

The better method is a combination of appointment and election. Judicial candidates can be nominated by the legal community of judges and lawyers. Nominations should be based on the candidate's experience and background. A panel of judges and lawyers can decide which of the candidates is most qualified. The public will vote whether they wish to accept the recommendation of the nominating panel, or vote for an incumbent judge.

The panel will make the qualifications of the candidate available to the public in newspapers and on the Internet. Campaigning for the election of a judge should not be allowed. Campaigns cost money. Campaign contributions are just another form of legal corruption. Those who contribute to the campaign are looked upon with favor, and that is what we are trying to avoid. Our goal is an impartial tribunal.

Once appointed, the judge should be graded on his performance. Lawyers and people who have had their cases decided before the judge should be given a form to complete at the end of the trial. The form should ask the person to rate the judge on such things as impartiality, knowledge of the law and courtroom demeanor. The form will explain that this information will be used to help voters decide whether to retain the judge at the next election.

No doubt some will say this system will not work because those who win will vote favorably for the judge and those who lose will rate the judge poorly. But I have seen a similar rating system in Palm Beach County, Florida, and it works. Lawyers are asked to rate the judges on performance. I found the results of the survey to correctly reflect my experiences before that judge. Bad judges were given low ratings. Good judges were given high ratings. Most were given a mix of high and low ratings.

Every four years, the judge should be up for re-election. Voting should be done as part of the presidential election. Elections held at other times of the year have a low turn-out. Holding the judicial election as part of the presidential election will get the biggest and most diverse turnout.

Prior to the election, the results of the ratings made by lawyers and trial participants should be made public through local newspapers and the Internet. The voters will be given a choice of re-electing the incumbent judge or voting for a candidate nominated by the panel.

Again, no campaigning should be allowed. The judge's re-election should be based solely on his performance on the bench as rated by those who appear before him. Now that is holding a judge accountable for his actions!

Thoughts For The Reader

I thank the reader for taking the time to read this book. My purpose in writing the book is to suggest ideas for the reader to explore.

I hope lawyers who read this book will realize that they have a major image problem. And this is not just my opinion. Consider the criticism levied against John Edwards — not because he did anything wrong as a lawyer, but just because he was a lawyer. How could he be a good guy and a successful trial lawyer at the same time? Lawyers can change their image by changing the way they practice. They need to strive to practice as Mr. Right and to put pressure on the Mr. Wrongs to change their ways.

As for the non-lawyer reader, I hope in the future he will expect — no demand, competent legal representation. A lawyer has a duty to put the client's interest first. The client should expect no less.

The final thought is the title of this chapter.
IT'S YOUR LEGAL SYSTEM. YOU CAN CHANGE IT.
And you can. Corruption starts at the top, but change comes from the bottom. That's you and me.

We may be at the lowest end of the political spectrum, but with our collective voice, we can change the system.

Glossary

ABSTRACT OF TITLE An *Abstract of Title* is a condensed history of the title to the land, consisting of a summary of all of recorded documents that affect the land, including mortgages.

AFFIDAVIT   An *Affidavit* is a written statement of fact made by someone voluntarily, under oath, or acknowledged as being true, in the presence of a notary public or someone else who has authority to administer an oath or take acknowledgments.

ALIMONY *Alimony* is court ordered payment made by one spouse to the other for support or maintenance while the couple are separated, or after they are divorced.

ANNUITY CONTRACT An *annuity contract* is a contract that gives someone (the annuitant) the right to receive periodic payments (monthly, quarterly) , etc.) for the life of the annuitant or for a given number of years.

ASSET An *asset* is anything owned by someone that has a value, including *personal property* (jewelry, paintings, securities, cash, motor vehicles, etc.) and *real property* (condominiums, vacant lots, acreage, residences, etc.).

ATTORNEY AT LAW An *Attorney at law* is someone who is licensed to practice law in a given state. In this book we used the terms *Attorney, Lawyer and Counselor* interchangeably.

BAR ASSOCIATION A *Bar Association* is an association of members of the legal profession. Bar Associations have been organized on the national level, such as the *American Bar Association*, on the state level, such as the Indiana State Bar.

BREACH OF CONTRACT *Breach of Contract* is the failure to perform a promise contained in a contract, without any legal excuse for failing to do so.

CLAIM A *claim* against the decedent's Estate is a demand for payment of a debt of the decedent. To be effective, the claim must be filed with the Probate Court within the time limits set by law.

COMPLAINT A *complaint* is the initial document that is filed with the court. It is a statement of the reasons for the filing and a request to the court for some sort of relief, such as ordering the defendant to pay money to the *plaintiff* (the person who filed the complaint).

CONFLICT OF INTEREST A *conflict of interest* is a conflict between the official duties of a fiduciary (guardian, Trustee, attorney, etc.) and his own private interest.

CONSERVATOR A *Conservator* is someone appointed by the court to manage, protect and preserve the property of someone who is missing, or who the Court finds is unable to care for his property because of age (a minor) or incapacity.

CORPORATION A *Corporation* is a company created by one or more persons according to the laws of the state. The company is owned by the *shareholders* or *stockholders*.

COSTS *Costs* are the out-of-pocket expenses incurred during legal representation.

CREDITOR A *creditor* is someone to whom a debt is owed by another person (the *debtor*).

DAMAGES *Damages* is money awarded by a Court as compensation to someone who has been injured by the action of another.

DEBTOR A *debtor* is someone who owes payment of money or services to another person (the *creditor*).

DECEDENT The *Decedent* is the person who died.

DEPOSITION A *deposition* is a means of discovering evidence that can be used at trial. It is a series of questions that are answered the presence of a notary public. The person answering the questions is called the *deponent*. He must swear, under oath, that the answers he gives are true.

DIY **DIY** is the abbreviation for "Do It Yourself."

ENCROACH To **encroach** is to trespass or intrude unlawfully upon the lands or property of another. A wall or fence which extends over a boundary is an illegal intrusion onto the neighboring property.

ESTATE A person's **Estate** is all of the property (both real and personal property) owned by that person.

EXECUTOR An **Executor** (or the feminine *Executrix*) are legal terms found in many Wills. The terms refer to the person appointed by the Will maker to carry out directions given in the Will.

FAMILY LAW **Family Law** is a branch or specialty of law concerned with adoption, separation, divorce, paternity, custody, support and child care. In some states it is referred to as *Domestic Relations Law.*

GUARDIAN A **Guardian** is someone who has legal authority to care for the person or property of a minor or for someone who has been found by the court to be incapacitated. See Conservator.

LAWS OF INTESTATE SUCCESSION The **Laws of Intestate Succession** are the laws of the state that govern who is to inherit the decedent's property in the event that he dies intestate (without a Will). In some states these laws are referred to as the *Laws of Descent and Distribution.*

LEGALESE *Legalese* refers to the use of legal terms and confusing text that is used by some attorneys to draft legal documents.

LIMITED PARTNERSHIP A *Limited Partnership* is a partnership created according to the laws of the state. Each *Limited Partner* has limited liability. Each *General Partner* has control of the business and is personally liable for all of the debts of the company.

LITIGATION *Litigation* is the process of carrying on a lawsuit, i.e., to sue for some right or remedy in a court of law. A Litigation Attorney is one who is experienced in conducting the law suit and in particular, going to trial.

LITIGATOR A *Litigator* (also known as a *trial lawyer*) is an attorney who regularly pursues law suits on behalf of his clients.

MALPRACTICE *Malpractice* is professional misconduct. It is the failure of a professional (doctor, lawyer, accountant) to provide services in the manner as that of an average, reputable member of that profession.

NEXT OF KIN *Next of kin* has two meanings in law: *next of kin* refers to a person's nearest blood relation or it can refer to those people (not necessarily blood relations) who are entitled to inherit the property of one who dies without a valid Will.

PERSONAL PROPERTY *Personal property* is all property owned by a person that is not real property (real estate). It includes personal effects, cars, securities, bank accounts, insurance policies, etc.

PERSONAL REPRESENTATIVE A *Personal Representative* is someone who is appointed by the court to settle the decedent's Estate and to distribute whatever is left to the proper beneficiary. In Louisiana, he is called a *Succession Representative.*

PLAINTIFF A *Plaintiff* is the person who files a complaint or sues in a civil action.

PRENUPTIAL AGREEMENT A *Prenuptial Agreement* (also known as an *Antenuptial Agreement*) is an agreement made prior to marriage whereby a couple determines how their property is to be managed during their marriage and how their property is to be divided should one die, or they later divorce.

PROBATE *Probate* is a court procedure in which a court determines the existence of a valid Will. The decedent's Estate is then settled by the Personal Representative who pays all valid claims and then distributes whatever remains to the proper beneficiary.

PROBATE ESTATE The *Probate Estate* is that part of the decedent's estate that is subject to Probate. It includes property that the decedent owned in his name only or as a Tenant In Common.

PROMULGATED INSURANCE RATE The *promulgated title insurance rate* is the rate for title insurance that can be charged in a given state. The state's Department of Insurance sets the rate, and then publishes a table of rates based on the value of the property.

RAINMAKING *Rainmaking* is the term lawyers use to describe their efforts to generate business.

REAL PROPERTY *Real property,* also known as *real estate,* is land and anything permanently attached to the land such as buildings and fences.

RECUSAL *Recusal* is the process by which a judge is disqualified from hearing a law suit because he has a conflict of interest or because he is biased or prejudiced against one of the parties.

RETAINER AGREEMENT A *retainer agreement* is an employment agreement between a client and an attorney. It describes the services to be provided. It may also include an agreement for the payment of costs and expenses related to the representation.

REVOCABLE TRUST A *Revocable Trust* is a Trust which can be amended or revoked by the person who created the Trust during his lifetime.

REVOCABLE LIVING TRUST A *Revocable Living Trust* (also known as an *Inter Vivos Trust*) is a Revocable Trust that is created and becomes effective during the lifetime of the person who created the Trust.

SLANDER *Slander* is the speaking of false words concerning another such that the person's reputation is harmed.

SOLE PRACTITIONER A *Sole Practitioner* is an attorney who practices law as a sole proprietorship. He owns all of the assets of his law firm and he is personally liable for all of the debts of the firm.

SUCCESSOR TRUSTEE A *Successor Trustee* is someone who takes the place of the Trustee.

TITLE INSURANCE *Title Insurance* is a policy issued by a title company after searching title to the property. The insurance covers losses that result from a defect of title, such as unpaid taxes, or someone with a claim of ownership of the property.

TRUSTEE A *Trustee* is a person, or institution, who accepts the duty of caring for property for the benefit of another.

UNDUE INFLUENCE *Undue influence* is pressure, influence or persuasion that overpowers a person's free will or judgment, so that a person acts according to the will or purpose of the dominating party.

INDEX

A

B

C

R

S

T

U

W

WEB SITES

Guiding Those Left Behind

Amelia E. Pohl has written a series of books explaining how to settle an Estate. Each book is state specific, telling how things are done in that state. Each book explains:

 ◇ who to notify
 ◇ how to locate the decedent's property
 ◇ how to get possession of your inheritance
 ◇ when you do, and do not, need an attorney
 ◇ the rights of a beneficiary, and much more.

Each book is written with the assistance of an experienced attorney who is licensed and is practicing in that state. The *Guiding* series is currently available for the following states:

ALABAMA, ARIZONA, CALIFORNIA, CONNECTICUT
FLORIDA, GEORGIA, HAWAII, ILLINOIS, INDIANA
IOWA, KENTUCKY, LOUISIANA, MASSACHUSETTS
MARYLAND, MICHIGAN, MINNESOTA, MISSOURI
MISSISSIPPI, NEW JERSEY, NEW YORK
NORTH CAROLINA, OHIO, OKLAHOMA
PENNSYLVANIA, SOUTH CAROLINA, TENNESSEE
TEXAS, UTAH, VIRGINIA, WASHINGTON, WISCONSIN

Visit our Web site http://www.eaglepublishing.com to check whether books for other states are available at this time.

SPECIAL OFFER FOR PURCHASERS OF THIS BOOK
$22 INCLUDES SHIPPING
To order call (800) 824-0823

A Will is Not Enough

Many people who have a Will think that they have their affairs in order. They believe that their Will can take care of any problem that may arise. But the primary function of a Will it to distribute property to people named in a Will. A Will cannot:

- ⇨ Protect your assets and limit your debt
- ⇨ Provide care for a minor or disabled child
- ⇨ Avoid Guardianship
- ⇨ Appoint someone to make your health care decisions should you be unable to do so
- ⇨ Appoint someone to handle your finances should you be unable to do so
- ⇨ Arrange to pay for your health care should you need long term nursing care, including qualifying for MEDICAID.

AMELIA E. POHL, Esq. has written a series of state specific books explaining how to do all these things.

A Will Is Not Enough is now available for:
ARIZONA, CALIFORNIA, COLORADO, CONNECTICUT
FLORIDA, GEORGIA, HAWAII, INDIANA, ILLINOIS
MARYLAND, MASSACHUSETTS, MICHIGAN
NEBRASKA, NEW JERSEY, NEW MEXICO, NEW YORK
OREGON, PENNSYLVANIA, TEXAS, VIRGINIA
WASHINGTON and WISCONSIN

Readers of this book can purchase *A Will Is Not Enough* for $25 including shipping and handling. To order or to check for book availability in other states call Eagle Publishing Company at (800) 824-0823.

Main   4/12

5/
1